kame
BOO

G000081432

www.kamerabooks.com

Colin Odell and Michelle Le Blanc

JOHN CARPENTER

kamera
BOOKS

First published in 2011 by Kamera Books,
an imprint of Oldcastle Books,
PO Box 394, Harpenden, Herts, AL5 1XJ
www.kamerabooks.com

Parts of this book were originally published as the Pocket Essential
John Carpenter

ISBN
978-1-84243-338-6 (print)
978-1-84243-497-0 (kindle)
978-1-84243-498-7 (epub)
978-1-84243-499-4 (pdf)

2 4 6 8 10 9 7 5 3 1

Typeset by Elsa Mathern
Printed & bound in Great Britain by the MPG Books Group

For Joan and John (aka G&G), with love,
even though they probably haven't seen any of these films

ACKNOWLEDGEMENTS

Our thanks for the usual distractions to: Paul and Lizbeth, Gavin and Hanako, John and Elli and Andy B. A big hug for Marika. Our love to Christine and Tony Le Blanc, Truus Odell and Marc Le Blanc and Vicky Campo.

Thanks also to Hannah Patterson, Ion Mills and Anne Hudson.

CONTENTS

JOHN CARPENTER –
AMERICAN AUTEUR

John Carpenter is one of Hollywood's most consistent story-tellers. He is an independent film artist with a strong personal vision, as well as a talented writer and composer and his name alone will draw people into the cinemas. Ultimately his reputation is built on one overriding talent – his ability to tell a story and tell it well, whether you are shivering at the Shape, rooting for Starman's return home, gazing wide-eyed at the grotesqueries of the Thing, singing with Elvis, grimacing with Snake or running out of gum with Nada. Those that label him a director of 'mere' genre entertainment are ignoring his role as torch-bearer for the continuation of formalised Hollywood narrative form, an art usually swamped by fads and a myriad of showy techniques in modern cinema. For over 30 years his films have entertained audiences but many have hardly dated compared with some of their contemporaries – *Assault on Precinct 13*, for example, looks as fresh as the day it was first screened; its violence is still shocking, its soundtrack still effective and both the dialogue and its delivery are top notch, all in a film whose $100,000 budget wouldn't satisfy the catering demands of the average Hollywood picture. This is because there is an overriding vision, a consistency to Carpenter's work that rewards repeat viewing and presents a single unifying world view. He is an auteur.

'In France, I'm an auteur.
In England, I'm a horror movie director.
In Germany, I'm a filmmaker.
In the US, I'm a bum.'

John Carpenter in SFX November 1996

The basis of *les politiques des auteurs* was structured, somewhat haphazardly, in *Cahiers du Cinéma* in the 1950s and expanded upon by Andrew Sarris, among others. Nowadays the term is either derided as naïve or used with abandon by critics who attach the label to any director they see fit. In *Cahiers'* terms, auteurs are those directors whose authorial stamp transcends the formulaic genre material with which they work. In some sense directors like Peter Greenaway or David Lynch are not true auteurs because their material is 'art' – these directors don't make 'popcorn' movies but pursue a personal vision with their material and its execution. Whilst Carpenter often writes as well as directs, he is, nevertheless, a filmmaker whose body of work is generally based in traditionally 'lowbrow' corners of the market – science fiction, action and horror genres. That he has worked with lower-budget films probably explains his description of being treated as 'a bum' in the US, but he has consistently shown that, when given complete control over a film (which is why commanding higher budgets is more difficult – studios are notoriously twitchy about allowing creative control with large amounts of their cash), the end results are worth the creative struggle in realising them. It is this integrity as an artist that has resulted in such a high hit rate of great movies.

'...the meaning of the film of an auteur is constructed a posteriori; the meaning – semantic, rather than stylistic or expressive – of the films of a metteur en scène exists a priori.'

Peter Wollen, *Signs and Meaning in the Cinema*

Carpenter's position as an auteur is evident following the cumulative effect of watching his films. They are distinctly *his* because of the control he has over their execution, and not a result of the scripts he has either written or been given to direct. To emphasise this it is worth looking at some films that he wrote but did not direct – any of these could have been made, by Carpenter, into a John Carpenter film. *The Eyes of Laura Mars*, *Black Moon Rising* and *The Philadelphia Experiment* all had reasonable budgets, respected actors, wide distribution and were based upon screenplays written by Carpenter. Not one of them bears the hallmarks of his direction. Enjoyable but disposable, they are the works of *metteurs en scène*, their meaning is constructed 'a priori' in the (often re-written) screenplays. Carpenter's gift lies in storytelling, in the dramatic way that he interprets the material and not necessarily in the material itself. On virtually every one of his cinematic films from *Assault on Precinct 13* onwards, the titles of his movies have been preceded by the tag 'John Carpenter's'; and with good reason, since he fights, and sometimes even pays financially with lower budgets, for this credit because he recognises the director's position as primary cinematic creator. This again points to why perhaps he is not so respected in America:

> *'Since most American film critics are orientated toward literature or journalism, rather than toward future filmmaking, most American film criticism is directed toward the script instead of toward the screen.'*
>
> Andrew Sarris, *Notes on the auteur theory*, 1962

With John Carpenter's films, the screen is undoubtedly the primary consideration.

GOTTERDAMMERUNG, PROFESSIONALISM AND OTHER THEMES

The question of auteurship, then, refers to those who work on genre films, i.e. those that are considered 'less worthy' of study as art, for example westerns and musicals or, heaven forbid, horror and science fiction. Carpenter works entirely in this marketplace, but what makes his films interesting is that he often blends elements external to the single genre to create a hybrid. In many ways he repeats the same few movies in his own inimitable style, but keeps the material fresh by approaching it from radically different angles. Thus *Escape from New York* (sci-fi/action/road movie) is completely different from *Starman* (sci-fi/romance/road movie) or *Dark Star* (sci-fi/comedy). Similarly there's *The Thing* (sci-fi/horror/siege), *Ghosts of Mars* (sci-fi/horror/siege) and *Assault on Precinct 13* (contemporary western/siege), *Vampires* (contemporary western/supernatural horror), *Someone's Watching Me!* (thriller/horror), *Halloween* and *The Ward* (thriller/supernatural horror). Almost all of Carpenter's output looks further than just the 'type' of film it nominally is; *Big Trouble in Little China* seemingly throws in every genre with glorious abandon and to great effect. This is why his films work; as an audience you can enjoy them as they comprise easy-to-understand conventions, but these conventions are manipulated and mixed to produce something altogether more interesting, unexpected and satisfying.

Because of the nature of Carpenter's themes and motifs, be aware that the following paragraphs – and the film commentaries – contain spoilers.

Carpenter heroes are often of the type characterised by his favourite movie director, Howard Hawks. They may have flaws to their characters, indeed many are anti-heroes, but they all show Hawksian professionalism – there is no universal redemptive solution and they cannot necessarily rely on others. The job well done sees its rewards on a personal level and does not need to be spelled out, because that would be superficial. In *Escape from New York*, Snake Plissken rescues the President against unfathomable odds but no one really gives a damn. In *Assault on Precinct 13*, Lieutenant Bishop's comforting but hollow words – 'You did good' – are met with the stern response – 'If I were any good she'd still be alive.' This mirrors Cary Grant's words in *Only Angels Have Wings* (1939) when dead comrade Joe is given the epitaph 'He just wasn't good enough.'

Occasionally, though, Carpenter twists the audience's preconceptions about the nature of heroism and the effectiveness of the individual to deconstruct commonly held ideals about male machismo. Jack Burton (*Big Trouble in Little China*) is one such parody and, to a lesser extent, Nada (*They Live*) is another. At the other end of the spectrum, the heroic male is taken to testosterone-drenched limits in the figure of Jack Crow (*Vampires*) who has no qualms about throwing his machismo around to achieve his aims, even if it does make him a deeply nasty individual. Women are usually treated as equals in Carpenter's films – Laurie Strode (*Halloween*), Stevie Wayne (*The Fog*), Leigh Michaels (*Someone's Watching Me!*), Leigh (*Assault on Precinct 13*), Melanie Ballard (*Ghosts of Mars*) and Kristen (*The Ward*) are all rounded, spunky characters; they are just as brave as any man, intelligent and capable. Leigh Michaels even talks witty, snappy dialogue that is reminiscent of Rosalind Russell in *His Girl Friday* (1940).

Carpenter never gives his heroes a break. The protagonists' situations are usually severe and extreme. Of course, in any film, it's necessary to set up some aim or adversary otherwise there's not much entertainment value, but Carpenter sets up circumstances that appear nigh-on impossible. In *Vampires*, Jack Crow doesn't face any old master vamp, he's up against the one who started it all. The supernatural entities of *The Thing*, *Prince of Darkness* and *In the Mouth of Madness* are ancient, even alien, beings, powerful beyond human comprehension. Michael Myers, a little boy at the beginning of *Halloween*, acquires unnatural characteristics and is seemingly impervious to pain. Even non-paranormal situations appear insurmountable, such as the trio facing an entire army of hoodlums in *Assault on Precinct 13*. Very often, the hero is the individual against the horde, or the individual against authority – sometimes both. There is a vein of distrust for authoritative figures and organisations, especially when they betray the people they are meant to be protecting. This runs most obviously in the Snake Plissken films, but can also be seen in the attitudes portrayed by certain, apparently moral, institutions. The Catholic Church is criticised in *Vampires*; in *Prince of Darkness*, the very basis of Christian faith is hidden by the Vatican elite; and in *The Fog*, the foundation of an outwardly respectable community is shown to have been derived from blood money. Kristen in *The Ward* has to endeavour to escape from the routines defined by the staff at a psychiatric hospital. The establishment is also ripe for criticism – as illustrated by the incompetence that leads to the release of Michael Myers, the fanatical self-interest of leaders such as the President in *Escape from New York*, and the conniving government conspiracies of *They Live* and *Village of the Damned*.

Possibly one of the reasons that Carpenter has remained relatively marginalised in Hollywood is that, despite their upbeat pacing and witty dialogue, most of his films end on a downbeat note. Even when the heroes triumph their victory is Pyrrhic; the protagonists have lost as much as they have gained. *Halloween* ends with the killer still at large; *Dark Star* (a comedy!) ends with the characters dead. Both Snake Plissken movies conclude with the human race facing, if not extinction, at least severe hardship, and *The Thing*'s ambiguous ending sees the survivors unsure as to their fate. Nada's victory over the aliens in *They Live* doesn't rule out possible retaliation but he's too dead to find out anyway, while *In the Mouth of Madness* shows the entire world going insane. Even *Memoirs of an Invisible Man's* 'boy and girl walking off into the credits' finds no solution for Chevy Chase's predicament. All this pessimism is anathema to Hollywood, which expects the audience to feel good leaving the cinema; but, paradoxically, the films never feel downbeat while you are watching them. The fact that the endings are rarely rosy goes some way to help the audience believe in the characters. They become more real because hardships don't magically disappear at the film's close and the heroes still bear the scars.

INTELLIGENT COMMERCIAL AMERICAN FILMMAKERS? I HEARD THEY WERE DEAD...

> *'Some directors put a stamp on their work and some don't. Some are good storytellers and some aren't.'*
>
> Howard Hawks

> *'As an audience member I have to identify with characters on the screen and the things that happen to them.'*
>
> John Carpenter in *Horror Cafe* (1990)

Carpenter is fond of predominantly 'transparent' cinema in that most of his shots are there for the purpose of telling the story. Whilst this may seem the obvious way to film anything, it is, certainly in modern cinema, something of a rarity – especially in the action genre. Carpenter's reputation boils down to the emotional connection between the audience and his characters. Hawks often said that his primary concern as a director was to tell a story and, for the most part, this is what Carpenter does too. This is not to say he follows Hawks's technique; instead he adopts the ethos, deviating from these ideals when necessary. *In the Mouth of Madness*, for example, has a fragmentary structure that is designed to disorientate the viewer. The current trend towards dizzying pyrotechnics and 'look at me' camerawork has little place in his oeuvre, as these ultimately detract from the tale. The camerawork is certainly not bland; it just doesn't draw attention to itself. In many ways, Carpenter brings modern technology and innovation to classical Hollywood techniques. Take the opening of *Halloween*, a technical *tour de force* and ostensibly a stylistic device, one of the first major uses of Panaglide in a feature film. Technical prowess aside, the shot simultaneously hides the identity of the killer (and, importantly, his age), implicates the audience in the viewing process as complicit in the killing (like *Peeping Tom* [1960]) but succinctly tells us about Michael, his sister, his motives and his psychosis. In *The Thing*, much of the technical advances are in the field of special-effects work. Instead of relying upon swift editing or shadow play, the camera usually remains impassive to record the astounding and grotesque events as they unfold before our eyes. In the scenes leading up to the effects sequences, Carpenter employs a more standard form of storytelling. The use of unflinching camerawork to reveal the atrocities ensures that the viewers stare in as much wide-eyed disbelief as the characters, which allows the audience to empathise with their predicament.

Generally, Carpenter films as economically as possible and does not reject classical Hollywood practices, such as the 180° rule. Indeed, much of his work relies on shot/countershot, track-in cuts and other transparent devices that enable full audience engagement but also offer him the malleability of time. The key to manipulating an audience is not to let them know you are doing so. Despite the proficiency of technique, the fluidity of the tracking (a Carpenter track, especially in *Escape from New York*, is a wonder to behold) and the elegance of the composition, you rarely gasp at the camerawork like you would, say, in a Sam Raimi, Stanley Donen or Dario Argento film, as this is simply not its purpose. There is one aspect of Carpenter's work that is impossible to ignore – his love of anamorphic Panavision. From early on in his career he has insisted on the format despite its additional expense and the technical difficulties – widescreen films are notoriously unforgiving when it comes to focusing and depth of field, as well as having a tendency to 'lose it' at the edges. Whatever the logistical problems of filming in widescreen, the benefits are manifold – Carpenter's pictures are sweeping in scale and vibrant in colour. For this reason alone, they are designed to be watched, first and foremost, in the cinema. Television cannot do justice to the richness of his canvas. To make matters worse, until relatively recently his films have tended to be shown on television in pan 'n' scan mode, where the composition of the image is compromised in order to fit snugly on a TV screen. His works that do play well on television are those designed for it: *Someone's Watching Me!*, *Elvis* and *Body Bags*.

As a director working in genres that particularly rely on tension and audience engagement, Carpenter has to employ certain techniques to elicit an emotional response. One such device is the act of depicting nothing. An empty room is ominous because cinema is generally concerned with action – emptiness represents suspicion or disruption of order. Carpenter uses the principle to elicit concern in the viewer and create anticipation. There are two main ways that he uses the device, the first to compound unease and the second to lead up to a revelation, be it plot based or simply a scare. Sometimes both are employed. *The Thing* has a long sequence of shots showing the empty Antarctic station, which builds up audience anticipation to expect something unpleasant to happen. In *The Fog* there are two major montage sequences showing the town deserted and silent after midnight – it makes the sudden jolt of the car horns and lights spontaneously bursting into action all the more jumpy. Similar shots are used in the opening section of *Body Bags*, there are rooms with possible intruders in *Halloween* and *Someone's Watching Me!*, and even in *Dark Star* we survey the ship passively prior to the computer malfunction revelation. *In the Mouth of Madness* has the silence of a town deserted during the daytime being broken by unnatural children with malicious intent. The visual absence of a known threat is sometimes more terrifying than the threat itself because, paradoxically, the revelation of a horror provides relief from the tension for the audience, replacing it with excitement and exhilaration. Also, the absence of a definitive horrific stimulus plays upon the viewer's darkest personal fears.

Carpenter tends to get the exposition in his films over with quickly, as to delay purpose can often hinder an audience's identification with the main characters. In *Escape from New York*, Snake's mission is explained at the beginning where it can do least damage to the narrative flow, but it also allows us to formulate further opinions on his character. Similarly, *Halloween*'s entire premise is given directly to the audience at the very opening and Kristen is thrown into the world of *The Ward* with virtually no backstory. Generally the themes are explained at the start but occasionally, for example in *Prince of Darkness* and *Vampires*, there are some intense scenes of exposition part way through. In the former, the theories drive forward the magnitude of the evil and compound the film's meaning; in the latter, however, the explanations of Valek's origins, while giving Jack his mission and providing us with a more rounded background, slow the narrative drive of the film, although it does result in a rare opportunity to empathise with an otherwise despicable character.

An oft-neglected area of film study is that of sound design, something Carpenter excels at, often using sound to make his films appear more expansive than their budgets would otherwise suggest. He mainly uses sound in three ways:

- As Mood: mood tones set up suspense in a scene. They often take the form of ominous bass drones, occasionally accompanied by continuous staccato rhythms, to prepare the audience for 'something'.

- As Jolt: sound often emphasises an action; even when a noise is diegetic (i.e. part of the film world as opposed to the score) there is often an additional element which reinforces events on screen. Accentuating the sound with a non-diegetic crash or shout is a staple of the horror/thriller genre but Carpenter's use of this technique is exemplary. Take the scene towards the end of *In the Mouth of Madness* where Sam Neill slowly walks through the burning asylum. A drone builds up tension, so we expect something to leap out at him, but instead the surprise comes in the foreground in the shape of a humanoid shadow passing in front of the camera. The accompanying accentuating note jolts the audience, but it doesn't result in a cathartic act of violence or relief at false alarm, so the tension of the initial drone remains right through to the next shot.

- As Tune: Carpenter is normally fairly dismissive of his work as a composer, citing that he uses himself because he's cheap and hits deadlines. This self-effacing stance doesn't really hold up in the light of some of the most distinctive and driving soundtracks committed to celluloid – with very few exceptions you can spot a Carpenter composition at a hundred paces. What sets them apart from the normal cinema experience is that they do not merely serve as wallpaper but enhance the action on screen; indeed, prior to recording the score for *The Fog*, Carpenter was convinced he had made a dud. The soundtrack allowed the film's intent to come through. We are not talking occasional dabbles either; most of the films feature his original compositions and those that do not (especially *Someone's Watching Me!*) tend to suffer because of this. The exceptions are *Elvis* (it's about Elvis Presley, after all), *The Thing* (which, despite being by Ennio Morricone, does feature a couple of passages that are Carpenter in all but name) and *The Ward* (Mark Kilian's eclectic soundtrack really enhances the foetid atmosphere).

CARPENTER COLLABORATORS

No commercial filmmaker can work in a vacuum and all projects require others' involvement, even if they are following instructions – film is, for better or worse, a collaborative process. The contention about the director being the auteur of a film often rests on the amount of control they have over the final product. Carpenter has stated that, if it were down to him, he would be responsible for every part of his movies (*Chic Magazine*, 1979), an impractical idea but one which has the appeal of a vision undiluted by others – Carpenter is one of the few directors (Robert Rodriguez, Russ Meyer and Shinya Tsukamoto are among the scant others) who maintain a hands-on approach to their work. Indeed, Carpenter's most satisfactory films are precisely those where he has asserted the greatest amount of control and normally been involved with many of the other filmmaking processes as well. With that in mind, there are a number of collaborators who feature prominently on Carpenter's productions, people he trusts and uses time and again to help realise his visions.

Probably the most frustrating part of the filmmaking process is the co-ordinating and financing. Perhaps this is why Carpenter has tended to collaborate with the same producers, often in partnership, to get a project off the ground and into production. Debra Hill (born in Haddonfield, home of Michael Myers) was crucial in the production of Carpenter's early films, co-writing *Halloween* and *The Fog*, too, and even returning to the old hits by producing *Escape from LA*. In the intervening time she produced films with such directors as David Cronenberg and Terry Gilliam but sadly passed away in 2005. Larry J Franco saw his run of Carpenter films cover the gamut of budgets, from the modest *Escape from New York*, *They Live* and *Prince of Darkness* to larger productions like *The Thing*, *Christine*, *Starman* and *Big Trouble in Little China*, also acting as an assistant director on all these films as well as having cameo roles in *The Thing* and *They Live*. Sandy King has acted in a production capacity on Carpenter's later films, from *They Live* to *Ghosts of Mars*, also executive producing the *Vampires* sequel *Los Muertos*. She is currently married to Carpenter. It is worth noting that, with a few exceptions, Carpenter has mainly collaborated with two cinematographers throughout his career – Dean Cundey, up to and including *Big Trouble in Little China*, and Gary Kibbe, from *Prince of Darkness* onwards.

Actors are central to the way that an audience relates to the screen. Kurt Russell is the quintessential Carpenter lead; he was an A-list actor in Hollywood in such productions as *Tequila Sunrise* (1988), *Tango & Cash* (1989) and *Backdraft* (1991), but it's his iconic roles for Carpenter that are so memorable – Snake Plissken, Jack Burton, Elvis and RJ MacReady. Another regular actor, normally in support roles, is the prolific Charles Cyphers, who started out as Starker in *Assault on Precinct 13* before playing roles in everything from *Elvis* to *Escape from New York*. With over 200 films to his name, Donald Pleasence added significant gravitas to *Halloween*, reviving the character of Sam Loomis over the series, even after Carpenter had left it. His performance as the snivelling President of the US in *Escape from New York* adds to that film's caricatured charm. Husky-voiced Adrienne Barbeau became a popular figure in early 80s cinema, appearing in films by Wes Craven and George A Romero, after featuring in a number of Carpenter productions, notably the tense TV movie *Someone's Watching Me!*, *The Fog* and *Escape from New York*.

Tommy Lee Wallace, long-time friend of Carpenter and a member of Carpenter's band the Coupe de Villes, collaborated on a number of productions in a bewildering array of roles, often on the same film – editor (*Halloween*, *The Fog*), sound (*Assault on Precinct 13*), art direction (*Assault on Precinct 13*, *Dark Star*), and even shot second unit work on *Big Trouble in Little China*. He also went on to co-write and direct the sequels *Halloween 3* and *Vampires 2* as well as co-write *El Diablo*.

CARPENTER'S INFLUENCE AND GENRE FILMS TODAY

Although Carpenter's films show a strong background in classical Hollywood narrative techniques, they have nevertheless often paved the ground for future filmmakers. Up until the early 1990s, a large part of Carpenter's output, despite the classical nuances, was ahead of its time or marked the origins of a trend. Although it wasn't the first film of its type, *Halloween* launched a slew of slashers in its wake and its influence on that sub-genre is impossible to ignore. *Escape from New York* (along with George Miller's *Mad Max 2* [1981]) inspired a wave of grungy, post-apocalyptic action films. *The Thing*, too, although a commercial flop at the time, is widely acknowledged as a seminal example of the genre and a *bona fide* classic – the talk of a remake and a belated computer-game tie-in a testament to its lasting effect when many of its more successful contemporaries have faded from the public consciousness. Similarly, *Big Trouble in Little China* was way ahead of the game – Hollywood would take some time to accept the glories of exaggerated wirework, the influence of kung-fu outside of exploitation cinema and particularly the deconstruction of the western male hero as seen in Jack Burton. At the time, action heroes were all about blood, body count and explosions. Adding comedy to the equation was just too forward looking – *Ghostbusters* successfully pushed the envelope a little; *Big Trouble* threw it out of sight.

In terms of cerebral horror, *In the Mouth of Madness* is still a hugely underrated film, and maybe it will remain an oddity because the genre has since moved in different directions. The same year's similarly (financially) unsuccessful *Wes Craven's New Nightmare* (1994) eventually ushered in the postmodern horror movement as typified by films such as *Scream* (1996), knowingly bringing the conventions of films like *Halloween* to a new generation – 'Don't have sex, don't do drugs and never say "I'll be right back"' – but perhaps *In the Mouth of Madness* was just too meta for a trend to develop. Creepy Asian horror such as *Ringu* (Japan [1998]) and slow-burners such as *The Sixth Sense* (1999) became popular instead. The gore-no boom of the noughties, featuring excessive gore and dwelling on the victims' suffering, followed. Thought-provoking horror was out. Of all genres, horror is the swiftest at reacting to new trends, as well as plundering its rich heritage, so there is still a possibility that *In the Mouth of Madness*'s complexity may be re-evaluated.

With CGI effects becoming more affordable and more ambitious by the week, modern audiences have become saturated with an endless stream of spectacle. So is there still a place for the more visceral, tactile worlds of John Carpenter's films? Some have dated, that is inevitable. Some effects work, while technologically advanced for the time, now appears almost passé or naïve. Generally, though, his films can hold their own – the very hands-on and intricate nature of traditional effects work remains impressive. It's a touch ironic that the cheap but imaginative effects of *Escape from New York* now actually look less dated than those of the then state-of-the-art *Escape from LA*, while *The Thing*'s in-camera prosthetic work and timeless matte paintings are still pinnacles of the non-digital effects world.

Cinema audiences – the 14- to 30-year-olds that make up the bulk of Hollywood's target demographic – have moved on. In an Internet age where attention spans are low and need for information high, languid pacing and minimal plotting are not popular in the mainstream and are generally reserved for aficionados. Modern audiences are used to being bombarded with images in an escalating appetite for instant gratification. Storytelling has been replaced with an avalanche of detail and backstory – not always a bad thing and certainly it allows for more complex narratives, but often this occurs at the expense of clarity. In this environment, with an insatiable desire for consumption and a paucity of new ideas, it is to older films that many – particularly genre – filmmakers are turning. It is testament to Carpenter's work that so many of his films have been remade – often by a new generation of directors who grew up enjoying his movies. A cynic might point to the Hollywood bigwigs leaping upon the reputation of an existing franchise; after all, why spend money marketing a new brand when one already exists? These 're-imaginings' (of which more later) take the premises of the older films and buff them up to appeal to contemporary tastes – by either adding additional plot elements (*Assault on Precinct 13*, *The Fog*), explaining everything with detailed backstories (*Halloween*) or upping the ante in terms of pace, action or violence.

Like many of his contemporaries, Carpenter has been producing less work as of late with studios often more willing to throw money at young neophyte directors than rely on old-school filmmakers. *Ghosts of Mars* tried to inject some modern sensibilities, along with a heavy-metal soundtrack, into the mix, but felt like an old-fashioned reaction to contemporary filmmaking. Much more promising was *The Ward*, which demonstrated that he could embrace contemporary horror themes and mores whilst using traditional techniques of tension and shock to elicit scares from the viewer. Maybe this blend of the old and the new will produce a roadmap for a better future for genre cinema. We can but hope.

ATTENTION,
INCOMING COMMUNICATION

John Howard Carpenter was born on 16 January 1948 in Carthage, New York and raised in Bowling Green, Kentucky. His father Howard was a music professor and session musician with many celebrities, including Frank Sinatra, Johnny Cash and Roy Orbison. Carpenter loved both music – an influence from his father – and the movies. He was fascinated by films, especially those of the horror/sci-fi genre, such as *It Came from Outer Space* (1953). He also loved comic books. He was inspired to try making movies himself using an 8mm camera that his father gave him when John was eight years old. His main influences ranged from Howard Hawks, John Huston and Alfred Hitchcock masterpieces to science-fiction and horror classics such as *Forbidden Planet* (1956) and *King Kong* (1933), along with some low-budget terrors from Roger Corman. Carpenter was not just interested in creating stories, though; he also experimented with special effects – using stop-motion photography in the Ray Harryhausen style or even going as far as to employ such techniques as back projection. Among these films were such titles as *Revenge of the Colossal Beasts*, *Gorgon the Space Monster*, *Terror from Space*, *Gorgo vs Godzilla* and *The Warrior and the Demon*. He produced some fanzines too, which he also illustrated, and was in a rock band. After attending Western Kentucky University, he managed to get a place at the University of Southern California (USC) where he would formally learn his craft as a filmmaker. USC is one of the most prestigious film schools and many contemporary directors gave course lectures – guests included Alfred Hitchcock, Orson Welles, Roman Polanski and Howard Hawks. In 1969, Carpenter worked on a short 16mm film called *The Resurrection of Bronco Billy*, about a man who wanted to be a modern-day cowboy. His involvement was co-writing, editing and composing, with some directing too. The film actually won an Academy Award for Best Short in 1970. Carpenter's next project was to be his Master's thesis, for which he teamed up with another student – Dan O'Bannon. The pair set about creating a science-fiction comedy called *Dark Star*. It was an ambitious project and self-funded. Friends were rallied for acting duties and scenery was appropriated from rubbish bins. Originally coming in at just under an hour it served as a graduation film for the aspiring filmmakers; but, armed with additional money, extra scenes were shot and the film extended to feature length. It took three years to complete, with investment from various benefactors. Indeed, the actors' hairstyles had changed so much in the intervening years that wigs were needed for various reshoots!

Dark Star (1974)

Directed by: John Carpenter
Produced by: John Carpenter
Written by: John Carpenter and Dan O'Bannon
Music: John Carpenter
Credits for: Tom Wallace (Assistant Art Director), Nick Castle (Camera Assistant)
Cast: Dan O'Bannon (Pinback), Dre Pahich (Talby), Brian Narelle (Doolittle), Cal Kuniholm (Boiler)
83 mins

> *'Don't give me any of that intelligent life stuff, just show me something I can blow up.'*

The Dark Star spaceship's purpose is a simple one: find unstable planets and blast them to pieces, creating areas suitable for human colonisation. Armed with an impressive array of semi-sentient bombs and the soothing, sultry voice of their computer, life aboard the Dark Star should be a bed of roses. Only it isn't. Morale is at crisis point, the crew have been in space for 20 years (three years in their own timeframe – it's a relativity thing), a freak accident has left Commander Powell dead (but occasionally chatty) in cryogenics, the sleeping quarters are currently out of action, forcing the boys to sleep in the food-storage facility, and a disaster has resulted in the loss of the ship's toilet paper. Tempers are fraying: Boiler is moody and violent; Doolittle becoming dictatorial as the new self-appointed leader; Talby's a recluse, staring at the stars from his observation bubble; and Pinback… well, Pinback has to clean out the alien. It seems the only person who's chilled is the commander. Perhaps the prospect of a new planet to blast could liven things up, so the course is set for the Vale Nebula. But a chance hit in an asteroid storm damages a vital communications laser, causing bomb #20 to think it's time to detonate. It's all the computer can do to convince him it's a false signal but he's clearly not happy with the situation, a matter exacerbated when he is called out again…

For sheer nerve and persistence, *Dark Star* is a hard film to beat. For less than $60,000, a student project had become a viable cinematic film, competing with large-budget Hollywood pictures that, at the time, were at the height of their mega-buck, mega-star phase. *Dark Star* gained cult status and has remained popular to this day because of its obvious knowledge of the science-fiction genre and the fact that it is very, very funny. The antithesis of every serious science-fiction film of the time, its humour comes from the reverence to every film it pastiches. Most significantly, the film's prime targets are Stanley Kubrick's *2001: A Space Odyssey* (1968) and *Dr Strangelove: or, How I Learned to Stop Worrying and Love the Bomb* (1963). The space walk sequences, the central computer being a neutral voice (half HAL) and the talking bomb going insane (the other half of HAL) are from *2001* while the basic premise is *Strangelove*'s. One of *Strangelove*'s key plot strands features a group of air-force men given erroneous orders to nuke Russia, with one aeroplane not receiving the command to rescind due to faulty communications. If, plot-wise and visually, the film derives from Kubrick, thematically it rides closer to the writings of Philip K Dick – with machinery that not only responds but argues back, the vague mumbling dead kept in cryogenic suspension spouting stream-of-half-conscious thoughts (from *Ubik*) and, most importantly, the philosophical arguments. When matters reach crisis point Doolittle is forced to take drastic measures – he must discuss phenomenology with a confused explosive in an attempt to prevent detonation. Thus an important discourse is brought about as Doolittle and #20 argue that any logical perception of one's surroundings can only be gained from stimuli that may, or may not, be false.

Having a small crew stuck in a confined area allows the tensions to fly and space madness begins to take hold. Carpenter has described *Dark Star* as '*Waiting for Godot* in space'. Boredom breeds contempt. When Pinback announces that he is actually a case of mistaken identity, the others could not be less interested. When Boiler asks, 'What's Talby's first name?' the reply is the strangely desperate 'What's my first name?' Chiefly, the film's purpose is to entertain and amuse, which it does admirably. When the crew report to the ship's log, the contrast with *Star Trek*'s Captain Kirk recordings could not be more pronounced – no sharp efficiency but lazy interjections, interruptions and a series of petty complaints. Pinback's personal video diary shows a coherent journal deteriorating into a stream of bleeps and censored images. Pinback (played by editor/writer/special-effects man Dan O'Bannon) is definitely the star of the show, a whining slacker. Despite the deadpan humour of his 'bouncing eyes glasses' as he attempts (and fails) to improve morale with some gentle ribaldry, his finest hour comes when he is given the task of cleaning out and feeding the alien. Although long, the sequence emphasises the drudgery of day-to-day chores with acutely observed comic detail. Pinback has adopted the alien as ship's mascot – 'When I first brought you on ship I thought you were cute' – but the alien is as disenchanted as the crew and escapes its pen. Pinback has to chase the errant being around the spacecraft. Having been beaten with a broom, crawled through ducts and shuffled along planks to reach his quarry, he eventually ends up on a narrow ledge slap bang in the centre of the main lift shaft. The alien attacks and the lift descends, leaving him dangling by his fingertips as the sadistic creature mercilessly tickles him. These scenes are intricately planned using an in-camera trickery that belies the film's meagre resources in order to convey a real threat of danger along with the comedy. After this, the escalation (so to speak) of Pinback's personal disasters gets more bizarre as he finds himself stuck in a lift gyrating frantically and struggling to get free while, for his listening pleasure, he is played *The Barber of Seville*. To further compound his ignominy, his subsequent fate at the hands of the lift's automatic cleaning system would not be out of place in a Chuck Jones cartoon.

Despite being a science-fiction film *Dark Star* is really about isolated characters forced into close proximity. All the crew have distinct psychological needs that mark them out as clearly defined individuals desperately clinging to the last vestiges of their lives prior to joining the Dark Star. Doolittle escapes from it all by playing his can and bottle-water glockenspiel. He may well have become power mad in the wake of Commander Powell's death but deep at heart he remains a Californian hippie, yearning for the surf. Talby has coped by withdrawing into his own world, observing the wonders of space and contemplating the famous Phoenix Asteroids that circle the universe and 'glow with all the colours of the rainbow'. That both he and Doolittle finally realise their dreams, albeit in the face of death, is because ultimately everyone gets what they wish for – Talby joins the asteroids, Doolittle gets to surf, while Pinback and Boiler want nothing in life, and end up with exactly that.

Clearly, for a low-budget film with such a high concept, the effects could not hope to match the blockbusters of 1974, let alone today's CGI-drenched efforts, but, surprisingly, they stand up very well and provide the film with much of its charm. Yes, the alien looks like a painted beach ball with rubber-glove claws; but it has something that 90 per cent of the CGI minions of *The Phantom Menace* (1999) lack – character. A short while after the audacity of the alien effect has worn off, you buy it as a character and cease to see it as a ball; the film's trump card is that it takes its silliness seriously. Similarly, the baking-tray/ muffin-tin oxygen pack on Talby's spacesuit and the blue freezer-pop chicken dinner just endears the plucky production further. The first bombing sequence (a particularly laidback #19, all too willing to oblige) and the Dark Star's subsequent hyperspace jump is a dazzling piece of effects work, editing and humour, as the released bomb drifts slowly towards its target while the Dark Star shoots as fast as possible in the opposite direction, coming to an abrupt halt when it has reached a safe distance. The subsequent explosion of light in silence followed by a wave of sound is another nod to Kubrick.

Dark Star's long gestation may not have been the easiest introduction to filmmaking for Carpenter and his cohorts but it is testament to the film's quality that it has remained a cult favourite.

THE SHAPE OF TERROR

Although well received, *Dark Star* didn't lead Carpenter straight into a juicy Hollywood directing role. He turned to writing to earn his living and created some screenplays – a thriller called *Eyes*, which eventually became *The Eyes of Laura Mars*, *Black Moon Rising* and a western called *Blood River*. His next stab at directing came courtesy of an investor who gave Carpenter a shot at another of his scripts and, crucially, allowed the young director full control on the film. To have final cut on a picture is incredibly rare in Hollywood. High budgets demand a certain degree of damage limitation but, with *Assault on Precinct 13*, the limited sum available ($100,000) allowed Carpenter this privilege early on in his career.

Assault on Precinct 13 (1976)

Directed by: John Carpenter
Produced by: JS Kaplan
Written by: John Carpenter
Editor: John T Chance (John Carpenter)
Music: John Carpenter
Assistant Editor/Script Supervisor: Debra Hill
Art Director: Tommy Wallace
Cast: Austin Stoker (Lt Bishop), Darwin Joston (Napoleon Wilson), Laurie Zimmer (Leigh), Nancy Loomis (Julie), Charles Cyphers (Starker), Martin West (Lawson)
91 mins

'There are no heroes anymore, Bishop, just men who follow orders.'

Anderson, California. Precinct 9. Sector 13. Saturday. 3.10 am. The nightmare begins.

The Street Thunder gang are a bunch of hoodlums who are more than a touch miffed when six of their top dudes are taken out by police marksmen in a shootout designed to recover some illegally appropriated weaponry. Now they swear a *cholo*, a blood oath, which seeks to exact gruesome vengeance on the forces of law. Lieutenant Bishop is on his first day at work and is supervising the night shift at Anderson police station for its last day in service. Ordinarily this would be the dullest way to start a career, but the lieutenant is a local lad made good and knows about life in Anderson. Sure enough, a 'busload of hate' arrives in the shape of three death-row prisoners. The cons and their screws aren't the only unexpected guests to gatecrash the lieutenant's Spartan station, for a middle-aged bloke smashes through the door and collapses on the floor. Who is this mysterious stranger? Well, he's an unfortunate who provoked the ire of Street Thunder by wasting one of their chaps with a gun taken from a dying ice-cream man. He had good reason, though, because they did blow his daughter away when she had the audacity to complain that her frozen dairy snack was regular vanilla instead of her preferred vanilla twist option. The gang now has a focus for their aggression. So begins a long siege as the seemingly endless hordes of Street Thunder descend upon the isolated building. Matters become desperate as the captives and their ammo supplies diminish, forcing the unlikely trio of wounded receptionist Leigh, copper Bishop and mad killer Napoleon Wilson to team up and make a stand against the relentless assault. And Napoleon could really do with a smoke.

Pseudonyms are rampant throughout Carpenter's work. Realising that too many occurrences of the same name in the credits can be detrimental to a film's distribution – because it looks cheap – alter egos begin to emerge. With *Assault on Precinct 13*, the editor is a certain John T Chance, a pseudonym for Carpenter. John T Chance is the name of John Wayne's character in Howard Hawks's classic western *Rio Bravo* (1959), upon which *Assault on Precinct 13* is ostensibly based. Carpenter takes the premise of Hawks's film, appropriates and modifies some of the dialogue and imbues his characters with typical Hawksian traits; but, crucially, he makes the film his own. Leigh is the epitome of the Hawksian female. As tough as the men, she does her job with professionalism, barely wincing when shot – such a contrast with Julie, who suggests giving the catatonic man to the gang to save her own skin. It is to Napoleon Wilson rather than Ethan Bishop that we must turn to find the Hawksian male – he is witty, intelligent and morally dubious. Despite being a killer, he is not shown to be a bad man but rather an anti-hero – regardless of how he has behaved in the past we respond to his stoic attitude. He shares many traits with his *Rio Bravo* counterpart, Dude, the difference being that Dude has difficulty rolling his cigarettes while Napoleon is just desperate to smoke one. He is the quintessential Carpenter male who would later be reincarnated in many forms over subsequent films, most notably Kurt Russell's Snake Plissken. Lieutenant Bishop is more similar to the hero of another film that *Assault on Precinct 13* resembles: George A Romero's seminal horror *Night of the Living Dead* (1969), which features a group of misfits fending off the attacking masses, albeit zombies in this case. The leading male is black, but Carpenter wisely steers clear of burdening the film with racial concerns that could so easily have hampered its focus. To this end, Street Thunder are conspicuously multi-racial; in fact, the only person who brings attention to colour is Bishop himself when responding to Leigh's question about how he takes his coffee. Additionally, Bishop notes that the mayhem of the first assault has occurred in 'the last half hour'; this half hour of the film actually plays in real time. At once there is an immediacy to the turmoil and an allusion to *High Noon* (1952), which similarly used screen time to reflect actual time. Other homages are present (Bishop's first experience of the law reflects Alfred Hitchcock's father sending him to a police station when he was young) but this is not to say that *Assault on Precinct 13* is in any way imitative or derivative. It is the work of an auteur who has studied what he finds enjoyable or interesting about the film form and has used these as templates for his own vision.

Despite the fairly large cast this is essentially a triangular relationship between Bishop, Wilson and Leigh – Cop, Criminal and Girl. They are the only characters to show true bravery, spirit and a lack of self-preservation for the good of the community. At the climax of the first major brawl there is a brief montage sequence showing the three shooting at the (offscreen) gang members. Chaotic and violent, it emphasises the fact that they are a team. The angles of their guns and the swiftness of the shots in normal narrative Hollywood cinema would suggest that they are actually shooting at each other, but Carpenter employs an Eisensteinian slant that enhances their camaraderie whilst subverting cinematic language in a way that is surprisingly transparent to the audience.

The scene that is most often remembered is that of the 'ice-cream man', which gained the film a certain notoriety on release, and it would be difficult to imagine it being green-lit in these more sensitive times. A plucky little girl buys an ice cream but is shocked to find it's not the right variety, so returns to the van for a replacement. Unfortunately, in the intervening time, the proprietor has been smacked around by some gang members and the little girl finds herself on the receiving end of a bullet. The scene is shocking for many reasons – the murder is unwarranted and motiveless, it happens during the day in front of something 'nice' and, most importantly, a child is killed. Further, her father, intense with rage, leaves her body unceremoniously strewn on the pavement while he goes about exacting bloody retribution. When he finally faces the killers, he lets off all six shots into just one gang member, who calmly takes the bullets as though being attacked by nothing more than a water pistol. We are not used to this way of thinking in a film – when the gang member finally falls down and dies there is a sense of relief that standard concepts of cause and effect have not been violated.

Assault on Precinct 13 stands out from the run-of-the-mill action flick due to its aestheticisation of violence. From the opening scene, where the six gang members are gunned down, we can see the barrage of techniques Carpenter has in his arsenal – cutting between different shooting angles, flashes of light, plays of shadow and the elasticity of film time. We don't need a reason for the slaughter – that can come later. The power of the scene lies in its visual expression. It sets the audience up for the rest of the film. The first attack on the station is a deliberately confused set of killings as the faceless horde try to work their way in. Were the film merely an endless stream of shootings, the whole piece could have easily become boring, but each set piece is filmed in a different style to keep the audience on their toes. Carpenter even manages some tense and macabre surprises – such as the moment we discover what happened to the telephone repair man. 'That's not rain,' comments one police officer...

Most memorable of all is the film's incredible synthesiser score, from the driving riff that opens the credits to the slow introspective mood music that accompanies the poignant moments. The main riff has proved influential on a generation of musicians, cropping up in many 80s and 90s dance tracks, as well as providing inspiration for the soundtrack of the Bitmap Brothers' computer game *Xenon 2*.

Filmed on a ridiculously low budget, the end results do not reflect this at all. Lean, tight and tense, this is assured and audacious filmmaking.

Surprisingly, *Assault on Precinct 13* did not do good business in America but became successful in Europe and remains a cult favourite. In particular, Germany took to the film and it became one of their highest-grossing pictures of the year. It was popular in England too, achieving acclaim at the London Film Festival.

Someone's Watching Me! (1978)

Directed by: John Carpenter
Written by: John Carpenter
Music: Harry Sukman
Cast: Lauren Hutton (Leigh Michaels), Adrienne Barbeau (Sophie), David Birney (Paul Winkless), Charles Cyphers (Gary Hunt)

'Every time I go outside I wonder if he's watching.'

Leigh Michaels is due for a change in her life. A new flat in the highly desirable Arkham Tower, a new city (LA) and a new job as a director on live TV. However, changes can bring about anxiety and Leigh has more reason to be worried than most. You see, in the tower opposite is a very obsessive and dangerous man who has a fixation that sees him bugging her apartment and gazing at her through a high-powered telescope. The last object of his affection, Elizabeth, ended up taking a nine-storey dive from her tower block. With the deeply sexist Steve calling for dates, it is not easy for Leigh to work out who is the pest and who is the deranged psychopath. Things take a turn for the worse when the lights keep playing up, the door of her flat is left ajar and strange parcels arrive, compliments of Excursions Unlimited. Suspiciously, Excursions Unlimited doesn't appear to exist but nonetheless supply an impressive telescope and several bottles of wine from their fine range of products. Naturally the police are unwilling to waste resources pursuing an individual who sends presents and booze, which leaves Leigh feeling extremely vulnerable, especially when she realises the voyeur has seen her with her new boyfriend. Unwilling to move from her bijou apartment, the only way to resolve things is to take matters into her own hands.

Carpenter's first TV movie owes more than a nod to the auteurs' auteur Alfred Hitchcock; indeed, he was taught by the master of suspense whilst at film school. This homage is evident right from the credit sequence with its bold parallel lines fading slowly into the criss-cross of Arkham Towers' windows, a take on Saul Bass's opening credits to *North By Northwest* (1959). Likewise, the tracking into the first present (a case wrapped in manila paper) recalls a similar scene in *Sabotage* (1936), an exponential zoom as used in *Vertigo* (1958) and assured use of point-of-view camerawork. Most obvious of all are the links with *Rear Window* (1954) where James Stewart watches the lives of his neighbours, until he becomes convinced that the man in the flat opposite has murdered his wife. In *Someone's Watching Me!* the voyeur is malevolent and takes the viewing process to extremes, even going so far as to bug Leigh's apartment. But this is still very much Carpenter's film and in many ways similar to *Halloween* in terms of the methods used to elicit an audience response. When Leigh finds her door is unlocked and suspects intrusion, we (but not she) see a figure running in the background inside her flat and into the lift. This creates suspense but Carpenter also uses the technique of shock – a sudden face at the window accompanied by a jolting musical flourish and a number of false alarms. All these devices are used in a more assured fashion in *Halloween*. Most tense of all is the sequence where Leigh's curiosity leads her to the basement garage, knowing that the stalker is there. She hides under a grating and watches upward as footsteps approach. As he stands on top of the grille, she tries not to make a sound. Has he seen her? After an interminable wait he walks away but not before, in a moment of nonchalant sadism, he flicks his still smouldering cigarette right onto the cowering Leigh. It's a scene mirrored in Halloween's closing act where Laurie hides in a cupboard, as well as in the birthing sequence from *Prince of Darkness*.

Leigh is a strong woman and this is what helps make the film so believable, as the stalk-and-slash genre normally relies on the victims being stupid or weak. A realistic and sympathetic character makes empathy easier for the audience. Leigh is her own woman and has a quirky sense of humour. When she starts a relationship she doesn't compromise who she is and accepts people for who they are – she has no problem striking up a close friendship with Sophie, an open lesbian. Interestingly, while she is the attention of unwanted advances, she is never sexualised by the camera. Sophie is similarly strong; her lesbianism is just part of her character and not a defining label – a bold but laudable move for a 1970s TV movie.

Someone's Watching Me! received a brief run in some cinemas in Europe under the title *High Rise*. Although the film was made prior to *Halloween*, it wasn't actually broadcast until after *Halloween*'s initial release.

Carpenter's next project came about after an approach by producer Irwin Yablans. He had an idea for a cheap horror film called 'The Babysitter Murders' where a small town is subject to the attention of a serial killer who targets, you guessed it, babysitters. Carpenter, working with Debra Hill, expanded this basic concept and suggested that it should be played out on one night, on a holiday renowned for its scary associations. The air of the supernatural sets it above the moral low-ground adopted by many of the pretenders to its splendidly jewelled crown. The writers made a decision to try to include as many scary elements as possible. To this end, Debra Hill provided most of the realism, basing matters on her own babysitting experiences and fears, while Carpenter concentrated on the supernatural aspects of the piece. The result was to become the biggest independent film of its time and one of the most influential horror pictures ever. They had a mere $300,000 and a short shooting schedule...

Halloween (1978)

Directed by: John Carpenter
Produced by: Debra Hill
Written by: John Carpenter and Debra Hill
Director of Photography: Dean Cundey
Editors: Tommy Wallace, Charles Bornstein
Music: John Carpenter
Cast: Jamie Lee Curtis (Laurie Strode), Donald Pleasence (Dr Loomis), PJ Soles (Lynda), Nancy Loomis (Annie), Nick Castle (The Shape), Charles Cyphers (Sheriff Brackett)
91 mins

Haddonfield, Illinois. In 1963, little boy Michael Myers is caught red-handed having just stabbed his sister to death with a carving knife. Naturally the authorities are unimpressed by his youthful bravura and consign him to an asylum for good. Would that it were that simple. Fifteen years later and Michael ain't so little any more; his psychiatrist Dr Loomis despairs that his patient is unreachable, mute for the entirety of his incarceration. Myers breaks out of the confines of his prison. His destination? Haddonfield. The time? Halloween. Preparations are being made in the sleepy town for trick or treating and, with most of the adult population apparently out of the area, this naturally leaves the older teenagers to look after the little 'uns and earn a few bucks in the process. Laurie is one such entrepreneurial spirit but, unlike her friends Annie and Lynda, does take her role seriously and stick with the kids she's meant to be minding. They, on the other hand, would much rather be making out with their hunky boyfriends. Sadly, they have made the wrong lifestyle decision, as their unbridled sexual fumblings have awakened murderous memories in Michael Myers, of that night when he permanently snuffed his canoodling sister. And tonight is the night he comes home...

> *'[In] a horror movie everyone starts loosening up and the more blood you bring out the more fun it is. The more people killed then everybody, the crew, is laughing and joking – it's like a picnic.'*

This is the film which launched a genre and formed the template for many, many horrors to come, so it is difficult to view *Halloween* objectively and in the context of the time it was made. The success of any horror film can normally be distilled into the effectiveness of its villain; Michael Myers may start the film as a murderous young boy but, after the prologue, the film goes to extraordinary lengths to convince you that there is not a shred of humanity left in him. His nemesis Loomis is crucial too; while his character is ultimately no use in apprehending Myers, he is essential in giving the audience information – his role is that of narrator. 'I met him 15 years ago, I was told there was nothing left. No reason, no conscience, no understanding even the most rudimentary sense of life or death, good or evil, right or wrong.' In draining Myers of his soul he becomes an any-horror, universally fearsome – the bogeyman, the Shape. Laurie is unwittingly thrust into the role of heroine. Both she and the audience (while watching the film) are open to suggestions that others find ludicrous – that there is a bogeyman and he (most definitely he) is out there. A common criticism levelled at the slasher genre is that it is inherently reactionary – the virtuous live while the 'bad', deviant teenagers get sliced up as punishment for their dalliances. It is often cited that, in *Halloween*, Laurie is the virtuous teenager and therefore the only one allowed to survive the attentions of the Shape. Compared with her friends Annie and Lynda (cheerleader, smoker) this is undoubtedly the case, but she is only more responsible than they are, not more virtuous. Sure she is still virginal but doesn't refuse the odd toke on a joint, even if she can't keep the smoke down. In this respect she is a 'good' teenager, one who is believable, not perfect, but sticks to her responsibilities. She does not ditch her babysitting duties the moment an opportunity for teenage partying manifests itself.

Despite *Halloween* featuring a number of onscreen murders, it is not a particularly graphic film. The scares are generally played to make the audience jump or feel uneasy rather than gross them out. Most of Myers' handiwork contains elements of the surreal that makes his killings more macabre but comfortingly outside of 'normal' violent experience. The jumps are accompanied by an accentuating sound to drive home the scare, a horror trick that is regularly used even now. Despite Loomis emptying a magazine of bullets into Myers, it is down to our plucky heroine, showing all her resourcefulness, to confront the killer but, ever the responsible one, she makes sure the kids are safe first. This professionalism puts her in the Hawksian mould – she does her job and she is gutsy but not perfect. That the Shape disappears at the film's close doesn't alter her role as a heroine but confirms Myers' position as a mythical entity.

Dean Cundey makes exceptional use of colour and shadows (including the now clichéd blue backlighting inspired by the unnerving look of Polanski's *Chinatown* [1974]) but the real star here is the Panaglide camera. Carpenter had been enthusiastic about using the Panaglide (or Steadicam, a body-supported damping system that enables a camera to move freely and fluidly) since he heard of the device. Placing the money behind the camera, *Halloween* looks a lot more expensive than it actually is. The end results are highly impressive for a technology in its infancy. The opening shot – actually two shots carefully edited when Myers puts on the clown mask – is remarkably fluid and complex. Taking a whole day to shoot, it is played entirely from young Myers' point of view, blurring the boundaries between cinematic voyeurism and empathy for the killer, as he approaches his home, watches his sister and her boyfriend making out, grabs a knife from the kitchen drawer, mounts the stairs, dons his mask and stabs his topless sibling before leaving and facing his parents. The audacious decision to show the scene in, apparently, one take was inspired by Orson Welles' opening shot in *Touch of Evil* (1958) but could also be seen as another Hitchcock homage in the shape of *Rope* (1948). Perhaps the clearest relationship between the film and Hitchcock is through the grandfather of all slashers – *Psycho* (1960). Indeed, Sam Loomis comes from the name of Marion Crane's boyfriend and Marion Crane herself was played by Jamie Lee Curtis's mother Janet Leigh. Mother and daughter would later appear in *The Fog* and *Halloween H20* (1997). The films shown playing to the children on Halloween night (although others are mentioned) are *The Thing from Another World* (1951), which Carpenter would later re-make as *The Thing*, and *Forbidden Planet* (1956). Both films feature killer 'shapes' which are otherworldly and inexplicable. Laurie has a James Ensor self-portrait on her bedroom wall, an artist renowned for his fondness for masks.

Filmed in springtime, the autumnal look was obviously not available (if you look carefully, most of the trees are luscious and green) so paper leaves were painted brown to give the piece the requisite feel. Budgetary constraints meant that these had to be reused, so by the end of the shoot they were pretty tatty. Another piece of cost cutting came with the all-important mask used by Myers. A specially constructed one would have been too expensive, so what could be cheap and horrific enough to spook an audience? The answer was chillingly macabre: a William Shatner mask... painted.

As influential as the movie itself was the music. The only contemporary films to feature such inventive synthesised cacophony were those of Dario Argento, whose scores from Claudio Simonetti and Goblin are like abrasive versions of Carpenter's. The shiver-inducing minimalism and drive, the rhythmic 'plinkings' of the soundtrack mixed with ominous synthesiser drones would result in many pale imitations. The time signature of the piece is unusual, which gives a further sense of unease and underpins the thrills. Carpenter claims that he was influenced by his father, who had taught him 5/4 time. Carpenter wrote and synched the whole lot in three days with the 'Bowling Green Philharmonic'.

Absolutely peerless in terms of suspense and technique, *Halloween* redefined the acceptable face of horror. It went on to break box-office records and the investment saw returns eventually topping the $75-million mark. It became the ideal date flick – scary enough for couples to need comforting cuddles, but not so brutal as to induce nausea. Unfortunately, in its wake came a slew of hugely inferior 'homages,' almost all of which lacked its subtlety and tension. Either they were just long and dull acts of cine voyeurism (*Don't Answer the Phone!* [1980]) or replaced cohesion and tension with gore (*Friday the 13th* [1980]). On occasion they were tense and violent (*Maniac* [1980]) but more overtly misogynist. Other films used the title as a source of inspiration, with any memorable date being used to plunder the sales potential (*Mother's Day* [1980], *April Fools Day* [1986]). Although *Black Christmas* (1974) was an earlier holiday horror slasher, it was Carpenter's film that gripped the public imagination.

More projects beckoned for Carpenter. His screenplay *Eyes* had been filmed as *The Eyes of Laura Mars* (1977). Despite initial involvement with the picture, Carpenter was not happy with the changes to his screenplay and disassociated himself with the film. Television-land beckoned once more...

Elvis (1979)

Directed by: John Carpenter
Written by: Anthony Lawrence
Director of Photography: Donald M Morgan

Cast: Kurt Russell (Elvis Presley), Shelley Winters (Gladys Presley), Bing Russell (Vernon Presley), Season Hubley (Priscilla Presley), Pat Hingle (Col Tom Parker) Charles Cyphers (Sam Phillips)

Las Vegas, 1969. It's 'do or die for Elvis', who is due to appear onstage for the first time in almost a decade. With rumours of an assassination attempt surrounding the appearance, Elvis works up the courage to face his audience.

Mississippi, 1945. Loner Elvis is bullied by a local ruffian for talking to his dead twin Jesse Garon and being a 'mama's boy'. Years later he's still being bullied, this time for his ridiculous quiff. A friend convinces him to enter the school talent show and his performance is enormously popular. Snapped up by Sam Phillips of Sun Studios after recording a song for his mother, his crooning becomes successful on local radio and entrepreneur Colonel Tom Parker becomes his manager, pushing him to stardom. As the hits keep coming, Elvis buys Graceland for his mother before starting national service. During his stint with the army she dies, and he meets a new love, schoolgirl Priscilla Beaulieu. They marry and have a daughter, Lisa Marie, but Priscilla becomes increasingly frustrated living with a houseful of his friends and his long absences while on tour take their toll. Eventually, she and Lisa Marie leave him. Meanwhile Elvis needs to 'feel those people one more time' and approaches Vegas for a triumphal tour...

One of the great actor/director teams – file alongside Oliver Reed and Ken Russell, Robert De Niro and Martin Scorsese, John Wayne and John Ford – began with *Elvis*. Kurt Russell had already had a connection with the King when, in an uncredited role at the age of ten, he delivered a sound kicking to Elvis's shins in *It Happened at the World's Fair* (1963). Little did he know then that he would later go on to play Elvis himself. Carpenter and Russell got on extremely well during the shoot and the resulting film was a smash when it was first transmitted in February 1979. *Elvis* became the highest-rated TV movie ever screened at that time.

Told predominantly in flashback *Elvis* wisely bookends the story of his life with his 1969 Vegas comeback tour, and therefore doesn't fall into the murky territory of self-parody, obesity and drug addiction that plagued his last few years. It ends on a high and provides an opportunity to play out a number of hit songs. The Elvis portrayed is the one that fans remember and makes for compelling viewing. It doesn't gloss over the more contentious aspects to his life, which are occasionally sordid, but means that we are treated to a balanced portrayal of the man and the myth, without being either reverential or salacious. We see Elvis fighting, shooting his television, hiring and firing his friends and colleagues, throwing tantrums and eventually causing his wife and daughter to leave him. For every act of philanthropy (giving lavish gifts to all and sundry) there is an act of petty spite or rejection. As much as he needs to hear the cheer of the crowd, he hates the fame – 'Shoot, I can't even go to church.' He remains a child at heart and what really lifts the film from the straight biopic is the disturbing, almost Oedipal relationship he has with his mother. These scenes are uncomfortably intimate and she dominates these moments as she dominates her son. He even changes his hair colour to match hers and declares: 'You're prettier than Marilyn Monroe.' When freed of the burden of a living mother, he can finally seek a relationship.

Throughout the film, the onscreen events co-ordinate with both the visual elements and the soundtrack. Elvis lives in the shadow of his dead twin, Jesse, so when we view Elvis alone he talks to his life-sized shadow, a representation of his brother. Similarly, the purchase of Graceland would generally be viewed as triumphal, but instead the soundtrack plays – with some irony – 'I feel so lonely I could die' from *Heartbreak Hotel* and his return home is accompanied by *Are You Lonesome Tonight?*

Comparisons with Steve Rash's *The Buddy Holly Story* (1978) are inevitable; both are well-made and fascinating movies about the rags-to-riches story of a rock 'n' roll white kid, although *Elvis* remains the more intellectually challenging. Both have exemplary central performances; Kurt Russell is Elvis the same way Gary Busey is Buddy Holly. In later films Russell would consolidate his A-list status by becoming a star, effectively playing Kurt Russell in 'Kurt Russell roles', but here he is the King – his mannerisms, the sneer, the wiggles and the 'thank-u-very-much' are perfect, although his singing voice was provided by Elvis impersonator Ronnie McDowell. Kurt Russell's father, Bing, played Elvis's father and Season Hubley, then Kurt's wife, played Priscilla.

Carpenter had met Adrienne Barbeau during the shooting of *Someone's Watching Me!* and they began a relationship. The pair married in 1979. They set up their own company, Hye Whitebread Productions but, despite a number of ideas for projects, nothing concrete materialised and Carpenter teamed up again with Debra Hill to make another horror picture, again with a new twist on the genre. Carpenter and Hill drove the length of California to find the right location and discovered that iconic lighthouse in Inverness, just up the road from Bodega Bay.

The Fog (1979)

Directed by: John Carpenter
Produced by: Debra Hill
Written by: John Carpenter and Debra Hill
Director of Photography: Dean Cundey
Music: John Carpenter
Cast: Adrienne Barbeau (Stevie Wayne), Jamie Lee Curtis (Elizabeth Solley), Janet Leigh (Kathy Williams), John Houseman (Machen), Hal Holbrook (Father Malone), Nancy Loomis (Sandy), Charles Cyphers (Dan O'Bannon), Tom Atkins (Nick Castle), George 'Buck' Flower (Tommy Wallace), Darwin Joston (Dr Phibes), John Carpenter (Bennett, uncredited)
89 mins

It's five minutes to midnight on the 20th of April, one hundred years after a ship was wrecked in the fog on Antonio Bay, lured to its salty demise by a campfire. Legend has it that, should the fog return, so will the denizens of the shipwreck, slouching from their watery graves to seek vengeance for their premature departure from this mortal world. The town of Antonio Bay is celebrating its centenary with a candlelit march and rather insignificant statue unveiling. As the witching hour begins, nastiness is afoot. As Father Malone finds out in his grandfather's recently discovered journal: 'Midnight 'til one belongs to the dead.' The crew of the *Seagrass*, currently 15 miles from shore, are brutally slain by shadows in the fog, which, as husky voiced KAB radio presenter Stevie Wayne is quick to question, 'rolls against the wind'. But these spooky occurrences are merely the *hors d'oeuvres* to the following night's main course of murderous maritime mayhem. After a day of shock discoveries, Nick and hitchhiker Elizabeth have had enough – they find a corpse on the *Seagrass* with its eyes stabbed out and its lungs filled with enough brine to pickle cucumbers. It then proceeds to attack poor Liz in the mortuary. But, as they and the rest of the town are soon to discover, when the fog rolls in no one is safe from the thrust of a dead man's hook. The eerie glow drifts relentlessly to wreak its misty revenge.

'Is all that we see or seem
But a dream within a dream'

Edgar Allan Poe

So opens The Fog, Carpenter's return to horror, which ignores most of the prevailing genre themes of the time, eschewing the gratuitous nature of most of its contemporaries, preferring to look to older films such as Jacques Tourneur's *Curse of the Cat People* (1942) and *Night of the Demon* (1957) or the Val Lewton-produced *Ghost Ship* (1943). The Poe quote indicates the film's stance; it is a fantastical campfire tale that moves like a dream during the hours of the night where the supernatural can seem all too real. We should not treat the film with any sense of reality – the tale is ghoulish, tense, scary and, in the cold light of day, utterly preposterous. Take the piece of driftwood that Stevie's son Andy picks up on the beach (having seen it as a gold coin). It provides shocks (it drips salt water onto her cartridges and explodes her tape recorder) and unnerves the heroine with mysteriously appearing portentous text but is basically another scare device with no logical pretext. It is a perfect example of the power of suspense to keep an audience rooted to the spot. As in *Curse of the Cat People*, the best moments are impressionistic rather than explicit; it's the play of light and dark, the shadows, the swirling of the all-enveloping fog that create the atmosphere. Just after Nick has picked up Elizabeth hitchhiking, the light from his van window casts a shadow of the cross on his face just prior to the glass imploding. Similarly, the death of the last soul on board the *Seagrass* is played out with just a criss-cross shadowed face of the final victim staring out of the void, an orange, backlit shape occasionally making its presence felt at the left of the frame.

Thematically, the film plays with the collective guilt associated with the founding of modern America during its short history; the sense that wholesome towns with their respectable middle-class inhabitants have roots in an unsavoury past. The townsfolk have lured the *Elizabeth Dane*, a ship of rich lepers, to its doom in order to steal its passengers' money. That the church should be the symbol of the town's murky past and its former priest a key collaborator only adds to this sordid history. As Father Malone observes, 'Our celebration tonight is a travesty. We're honouring murderers.' Malone is an alcoholic but, in a Hawksian way, this flaw hides the fact that he is an honourable man. He is willing to give his life for the town and to atone for the sins of his ancestors. Naturally, the conflict between professionalism and alcoholism requires that he doesn't survive the proceedings unscathed.

The zombie ship hands are as dissected as their victims become, just silhouettes or hands and hooks in the fog. Ironically, the fog is a source of light in the darkness of a town deprived of electricity, streaming through doors and windows, further obscuring the menace, making it all the more intangible, all the more frightening. When Andy's babysitter, Mrs Kobritz, is hacked to death, the suspense is unbearable, the denouement swift, the descent of the grey, hook-wielding shadows onto her (offscreen) body shocking for its brutality in the sense that the violence appears unmotivated, is levelled at a geriatric and comprises a number of sickening squelches. It's the other side of the coin to the little girl's killing in *Assault on Precinct 13*. Unfortunately, this subtle nastiness cannot sustain the film's sudden and unsatisfactory close. Father Malone realises that, to prevent the town being terrorised further, he must return the stolen gold to the fog-bound dead. These have previously consisted of half-seen shapes, but now they become corporeal in the form of red-eyed swashbucklers shambling up the church aisle. Rather like the similarly smoke-obsessed *Night of the Demon*, the ending is slightly compromised by showing what we had already imagined to be far worse; the actuality doesn't match the expectation. The shot of a maggot-ridden, green-faced zombie attacking Stevie actually detracts from the overall horror. But this is a minor concern in what is fundamentally an enjoyably spooky chiller.

Carpenter's visual style is balanced by its careful use of sound, emphasised by his heroine Stevie being a disc jockey for her self-financed radio station. The contrast between the laidback, cocktail-lounge music of KAB and the sudden jolts, smashes and screeches of the spooky happenings provides the necessary tension and scares, further enhanced by layers of phasing synthesiser drones. When the hook-wielding zombies perform their murderous deeds, the sound actually shocks more than the visuals. The relentless knocking at the doors of their victims has a similar effect to that of Robert Wise's *The Haunting* (1963)

– simple sounds that make use of the audience's imagination to provide the scares. For such a relatively inexpensive movie, the effects still stand up, even 30 years on. Part of this is due to the subtlety of the effects – the suggestion of the unknown, rattling bottles, the breaking of glass or squeaky, swinging signs. The fog that engulfs the town is a wonderful bank of glowing eeriness. The film was mainly shot in Point Reyes, which is naturally foggy, but dry ice, clever lighting and Dean Cundey's camerawork enhance the effect.

The characters Tommy Wallace, Nick Castle and Dan O'Bannon are named after Carpenter collaborators; indeed, Wallace appears in the film as one of the ghosts. One of the bands playing on the radio is the Coupe De Villes – Carpenter, Nick Castle and Tommy Wallace's band. You can see them perform in Castle's quirky fantasy film *The Boy Who Could Fly* (1986).

For the slim 90 odd minutes that you are in the cinema, *The Fog* holds on so tight it never lets go. It is tense and spooky, but once the lights have come up its horror disperses just like the mist itself.

The Fog was an unqualified success on release, both at the box office and critically. Carpenter now had a reputation for bringing in profit for low-budget features. Avco Embassy were next in line to offer him work, this time a cool $7 million for a film he had started writing some years before. Teaming up again with Debra Hill and Nick Castle, they came up with the script for a science-fiction adventure with a twist. Carpenter was keen to have Kurt Russell aboard and also managed to persuade Donald Pleasence to put in an appearance.

Escape from New York (1981)

Directed by: John Carpenter
Produced by: Debra Hill and Larry Franco
Written by: John Carpenter and Nick Castle

Director of Photography: Dean Cundey
Music: John Carpenter with Alan Howarth
Cast: Kurt Russell (Snake Plissken), Adrienne Barbeau (Maggie), Donald Pleasence (President), Harry Dean Stanton (Harold Hellman aka Brain), Isaac Hayes (The Duke), Lee Van Cleef (Hauk), Ernest Borgnine (Cabbie), Charles Cyphers (Secretary of State), Season Hubley (Girl in Chock Full O'Nuts)
99 mins

New York. 1997. Not a buzzing metropolis of designer shops and Broadway musicals but a city which, for the best part of a decade, has been contained by high-security walls and patrolled with deadly efficiency by missile-shooting helicopters. America's crime problem has become so bad that any criminal is thrown into the rotten core of the Big Apple, to fend for themselves among their convicted perpetrator peers: 'The rules are simple – once you go in, you don't come out.' A new arrival in this penal city is the notorious 'Snake' Plissken, one-time decorated war hero turned robber. However, he'll get a pardon should he take on a potentially dangerous mission to rescue the President ('President of what?' – 'It's not funny, Plissken') from the clutches of the Duke, the leader of New York's internal crime gang who has the jittery statesman at his mercy following a hijack. How do they know that the Duke's got him? Well, the Duke's right-hand man gives the authorities the finger, the President's finger that is. The bad news is that Snake has only 24 hours to accomplish the rescue as the President needs to deliver an important pre-recorded speech for a Summit Meeting. To add a touch of impetus, the authorities thoughtfully place pinhead charges in Snake's neck. If they aren't neutralised by the time the broadcast needs airing then – kaboom! – no more Mr Plissken. Gliding into New York and landing on the top of the World Trade Center is the easy part; he is armed with a gun, a convenient *Gemini Man*-style countdown watch and a locator set to trace the President's own chunky bracelet. New York is big and unfriendly – who can he trust in a city of criminals? Mild- mannered jazz cabby Cabbie with his warming collection of Molotov cocktails? Gadget-man Brain? Brain's equally smart girlfriend Maggie? All of them want out and the President looks like their only ticket. For Snake, it's hours to either freedom or death, but, hey, we'd heard he was dead anyway.

While few would argue that *Escape from New York* is Carpenter's most accomplished film, there is a lot to be said for it being amongst his most enjoyable works – it is, in a nutshell, pure essence of entertainment. Carpenter is at his best when he mixes genres and *Escape from New York* blends the science-fiction action genre with, of all things, a road movie, resulting in an exuberant, vibrant and unashamedly trashy mix of Wim Wenders' *Kings of the Road* (1976), Walter Hill's *The Warriors* (1979) and any Ken Russell film you care to mention. There's even a musical number. Key to the film's success is its premise and the containment of the film in one place – like *Dark Star*'s space ship and *Assault on Precinct 13*'s police station – that emphasises the goal: to escape from New York.

After Russell's incredible performance as *Elvis* he and Carpenter became good friends, and casting him as the lead was an inspired choice. Not only does Russell fit this role perfectly, it virtually sets up every action role he has played subsequently. Snake, with his characteristic eye patch and tattoo that unsubtly emanates from his trousers, hisses most of his dialogue through teeth half-clenched in anger. He is a classic protagonist, a hard-working patriot who has been betrayed by his country, a rogue who, despite his avowed self-interest, does work for the good of others – an anti-hero and a professional. The duel aspects of his character are represented visually when he first meets Hauk – the top half of his body in the dark, the bottom in the light, yin and yang. Of course, they need a man like him; no one else would be brave, reckless or stupid enough to complete the mission. There is a sense in which Snake wants to help his country and believe in its leaders, but he knows deep down that they will betray not only him, but all the normal folk who died for the President's lousy tape. The tape itself is a MacGuffin, ostensibly the reason for Plissken's mission but of no consequence to the outcome of the story. The disposal of the tape at the film's close is not just a pun or a comeuppance but also Plissken's final rejection of his country's ability to inspire loyalty. For all his seemingly bravura attitude towards politics at the opening ('I don't give a fuck about your war, or your President'), his situation forces him to reconsider his political outlook. Similarly, whilst the communists who hijack Air Force One are caricatures, they do have a valid point about the political system and the President's attitude towards his citizens – when the President enters the only life pod, his final remark as the only person who at least has a chance of survival is 'God save me'.

The road-movie structure means that, in some respects, *Escape from New York* comprises a series of extended set pieces which, while adding to the overall colour of the film, do little to advance the plot. Most of what we need to know is covered in the opening act prior to Plissken's landing in New York, with the rest of the story running towards a conclusion that is succinctly signposted – either the President gets out or he doesn't. This is not a criticism as each of the set pieces fleshes out the future world with more detail (such as some cars running on steam or the rudimentary lighting) and increases the urgency concerning Snake's tight deadline. When Snake and Brain take an unfortunate detour through Broadway (introduced via a sideways track revealing a severed head on a parking meter), we have our suspicions confirmed about the dog-eat-dog life of most of the inmates. The pack of underground dwellers who rise from the sewers to terrorise the streets are called Crazies, a possible reference to George A Romero's *The Crazies* (1973), another film that is critical of governmental interference in the freedom of the populace. They have become mob packs, reactionaries that attack in groups because they can, sullied by their own apathy. Not so the Duke: his ostentatious car – with chandeliers for headlights and a glitter ball – prowls through the city. He is the Duke of New York, A-Number One, but like a cat he asserts his authority by playing with his prey. The tension between the characters makes the rescue attempt more interesting as we are never quite sure if any of the heroes are going to double cross each other. Brain has run out on Snake before and even gives him up to the Duke (albeit with very little choice) so we never know where our loyalties lie. That ultimately he proves to be sound and that his girlfriend is loyal and brave is irrelevant. The only person we are sure about is the President, a snivelling, self-obsessed politician.

Not only is this great fun as a film, it's a veritable 'who's who' of classic western genre stars and cult film favourites, including Harry Dean Stanton (star of *Repo Man* [1983] and *Paris, Texas* [1983]), Donald Pleasence (*Halloween*, of course, and *The Great Escape* [1963], who at one point in *Escape from New York* is dressed in drag for the Duke's amusement – reminiscent of his role in Polanski's surreal thriller *Cul De Sac* [1966]), Ernest Borgnine (Sam Peckinpah's seminal revisionist western *The Wild Bunch* [1969]), Lee Van Cleef (Sergio Leone's *Dollars* trilogy, *Gunfight at the OK Corral* [1957]) and Isaac Hayes (responsible for the hugely influential *Shaft* [1971] score and being Chef on South Park).

We are also treated to one of Carpenter's most memorable scores, a relentlessly driving collection of rhythmic pounding synthesisers that carry the action ever forward. Despite the repetitive nature of the many themes, the complexity of some of the rhythms is quite remarkable. The climactic race across the bridge is perfect in its intensity, emphasising the pace of the chase and overlaid with reverberating chimes that echo the metallic corpses of cars that litter the route.

Plissken's flight to the World Trade Center is partly shown through apparently computer-generated displays as he glides towards his destination. At the time, such effects would have been prohibitively expensive for a film of its budget and it would be some years before even such basic CGI would become commonplace. The solution? These scenes comprised models of the city, painted black, and reflective tape was used to represent the vertices. One of the technicians behind the effects was none other than Jim (now credited as James) Cameron who later went on to make *Terminator* (1984), *Aliens* (1986) and the all-conquering *Titanic* (1998). The rest of the effects are similarly well handled with some lovely matte painting work – particularly the impressive introduction to New York's futuristic skyline with a stunning crane shot.

Escape from New York is a hugely enjoyable romp that proved to be not only financially lucrative, but also spawned a number of imitators as well as a belated sequel.

HOLLYWOOD CALLING

Another success at the box office, *Escape from New York* meant that Carpenter was hot property. Despite the fact that he and Debra Hill hadn't really envisaged a sequel to *Halloween*, the prospect of one was on the cards because the financiers were keen to cash in on its enormous popularity. They decided to write *Halloween 2*, which follows straight on from the events of that night, in order to maintain some control over the project, but the director Rick Rosenthal didn't manage to emulate the tension, suspense and ambiguity of the original; indeed, Carpenter re-shot some sequences. His next stab at directing was to be a project funded by Universal Studios – a remake of Howard Hawks's *The Thing from Another World*.

The Thing (1982)

Directed by: John Carpenter
Produced by: David Foster and Lawrence Turman
Written by: Bill Lancaster
Director of Photography: Dean Cundey
Music: Ennio Morricone
Cast: Kurt Russell (MacReady), A Wilford Brimley (Blair), TK Carter (Nauls), David Clennon (Palmer), Keith David (Childs), Richard Dysart (Dr Copper), Charles Hallahan (Norris), Peter Maloney (Bennings), Larry Franco (Norwegian Passenger With Rifle)
109 mins

A lovely dog bounding through the snow. Sounds like a scene from *Lassie Come Home*, but Lassie wasn't being chased by two frantic Norwegians in a helicopter trying their hardest to pound the hound. However, the Scandinavian canine assassins have their murderous plans nipped in the bud and end up being chargrilled, having accidentally blown up their 'copter just feet away from an American Antarctic research camp. Unfortunately, despite its shaggy, husky appearance, it wasn't a dog at all but an extra-terrestrial carnivorous xenomorph thawed out after many thousands of years hibernating in the permafrost. Naturally, such a fiery entrance piques the curiosity of the American team and a small party heads to the Norwegian base to see what all the fuss was about. When they get there the sight that greets them is not pleasant: all the remaining Norwegians are dead, the only indication of their appalling end some video footage of an excavation. On their return it becomes clear that the mutt is a mutant, especially when it turns into a mass of tentacles and lashes around the cage like a screaming monster from Hades. Parasitic puppies are bad enough but when attentions rise further up the evolutionary ladder things start getting seriously out of hand. Slowly it begins to dawn on the team that what they are up against is capable of assimilating its victims and appearing exactly like them. So then the only question that remains is: who is human and who is not...?

'The further we get from reality the more power you have over the audience.'

The Thing had been made previously as *The Thing from Another World* (1951) by director Christian Nyby, although it is usually attributed to its producer Howard Hawks. In the original the monster is kept offscreen for much of the running time and revealed to be vegetable-based (leading to the immortal line: 'An intellectual carrot – the mind boggles'). Despite its low budget, it is a surprisingly effective chiller, only floundering slightly at the end when the monster is finally revealed to be a guy in a costume. *John Carpenter's The Thing* manages to keep the tension of the original but also shows us the Thing itself in unflinching and remarkably graphic detail – this is certainly no vegetable man. In developing the screenplay, Carpenter went back to the original source of Hawks's film, the short story *Who Goes There?* (1938) by John W Campbell Jr (under the pseudonym Don A Stuart), where the creature had the ability to change its form to mimic its prey. It becomes, in Carpenter's words, 'the study of the effects of fear on a human being.'

In the classic text *Hitchcock by Truffaut*, Hitchcock explains the difference between surprise and suspense by reference to a hypothetical film scenario involving a bomb under a table in a restaurant. In one film the audience is unaware of the bomb, in the other they are not: 'In the first case we have given the public fifteen seconds of surprise at the moment of the explosion. In the second we have provided them with fifteen minutes of suspense. The conclusion is that wherever possible the public must be informed.'

Hitchcock's perceptions on the difference between surprise and suspense are acute but sometimes the surprise is what an audience wants in a film – the quick thrill of an adrenaline rush. *The Thing* manages to pull off both the suspense and the surprise – in many ways proving to be the perfect combination for a horror film. The heart-starting scene, for example, plays so well, despite initially comprising only a brief shock, because it escalates to increasingly grotesque levels. When Norris suddenly has a seizure, his colleagues attempt to jump-start his heart. The perilous nature of the situation works as a perfect means of misdirection; our expectations, and those of the surviving crew, are that a man incapacitated couldn't possibly be the Thing. Wrong. The defibrillator and the doctor's hands holding it plunge deep into the chest cavity, whereupon the ribs become a row of teeth and bite the hands off. The monster corpse on the slab proceeds to thrash around, its neck elongating, the skin and veins ripping until the head plops onto the floor. The tongue shoots out, wrapping itself around a table leg and dragging it across the floor before finally sprouting arachnid legs and scuttling off. Later on, Carpenter employs both suspense and surprise to great effect when MacReady begins testing the blood of the survivors to see which of them is the Thing. We, and the crew, know that *someone* is the Thing but have no idea who. As the searing metal tests each team member's blood sample, the Antarctic wind howling in the background, the tension rises to unbearable levels as the possibility that the next one will be the impostor increases. Finally, of course, the creature is revealed and, as in the chest-burster sequence, we are treated to an extension of the basic jump as matters become increasingly gory and bizarre. This gives *The Thing* its real strength: instead of one shock you get suspense-surprise-grotesque – three for the price of one. Carpenter also ends the scene with a humorous line, to relieve tension… but only temporarily.

Kurt Russell said of *The Thing* at the time, 'You know it reminds me of the Disney films I did when I was younger. More gruesome, sure, but you never know how the creature is going to react' (*Twilight Zone* magazine, March 1982). He is right. Part of the appeal of the film is that it remains in an otherworldly context. By isolating the group in the harsh whiteness of Antarctica there is no real indication of when the film is set; despite the opening caption that states it is contemporary, it remains timeless. *The Thing* itself is a science-fiction entity beyond our comprehension, a primordial threat, like an intergalactic Grendel. Perhaps this is why, despite the viscera, the film was not censored – it is a monster movie and not a tangible horror, so far beyond everyday experience or expectation that it presents no actual threat. *The Thing* is the first part in what Carpenter calls his Apocalypse Trilogy. Its outlook is surprisingly bleak despite the fact that the film is really an old-fashioned monster movie. The simulation of the growth of the Thing, were it to reach a populated area, sees the assimilation of all life within 27,000 hours (about three years), annihilation through absorption. At the film's close we are unsure as to whether Childs and MacReady are who they seem and, if they are not, whether they will reach a populated area anyway. The question of the alien spaceship remains – the creature that caused the devastation came from a pod some distance from (what we assume is) the mother ship. What remains to be discovered aboard the larger vessel?

In realising the incredible range of effects no stone was left unturned, although most of the work was done in-camera – often at some physical risk to the cast and crew. The neck-stretching shot originally ended up in a blaze of toxic chemicals and a need to re-shoot, while most of the fire-fighting scenes were played for real. Part of the epic look of the film is thanks to the detailed matte work executed by Albert Whitlock – notably the discovery of the alien spaceship. Whitlock had created the matte paintings for Hitchcock's *The Birds* (1963), the highly under-rated *Marnie* (1964) and *Torn Curtain* (1966). Meanwhile, the mutant dog sequence was realised by the then newly formed Stan Winston Workshop, which created a sticky vision by use of an animatronic puppet. Effects man Rob Bottin, who had previously collaborated with Carpenter on *The Fog*, was working non-stop to keep on top of the multitude of graphic work on show, using everything from latex to bubble gum and melted plastic to visualise the unthinkable. The surprisingly creepy title sequence (which harks back to Hawks's original) was a relatively simple effect involving an animation cell, a fog-filled fish-tank, some back-lighting and a burning plastic bin liner! Partly to appease the studios, an extended final sequence was shot which depicted MacReady unequivocally surviving the ordeal, returning to civilisation and receiving a clean bill of health. Whilst in keeping with upbeat Hollywood endings, this would have betrayed the feelings of mistrust, tension and paranoia of the previous 100 minutes, so was wisely dropped. What also doesn't remain is a longer version of the climactic battle. Originally, the sequence was to have included more extensive stop-motion work to show a mutant hound bursting from the serpentine base of the rampant creature, but these shots were dropped in the final edit, not because of their quality but due to almost imperceptible matching differences between stop-frame and prosthetic work.

A classic combination of scary, shocking and gross, it may have been a long time coming but *The Thing*'s place in the annals of horror and science fiction has finally been assured.

The Thing was a surprising flop. This was probably the result of a release that coincided with *ET: The Extra Terrestrial* (1982). An R-rated film stood absolutely no chance in the face of such family-friendly fodder and it sank. It probably didn't help that its opening involves a bunch of guys in a helicopter trying to shoot a dog. Over the years (and over the Pond; it performed better in Europe) its reputation has grown, and it's now appreciated as a classic horror. Even today you can buy a variety of plastic figures featuring gross bits from the film and there is a computer game that succeeds in emulating the combination of tension, scares and group mistrust. But in 1982 things were very different. Carpenter was expecting huge returns from *The Thing* and plans were afoot to team him with another big name in horror – Stephen King. The Stephen King phenomenon was really hitting its stride at the time, and what better film for Carpenter to handle than *Firestarter*, King's novel of a pyrokinetic girl unleashing molten death against a government that treats her and her father as lab rats? It seemed to be the perfect choice of project, but when the box-office returns from *The Thing* were released, Mark L Lester got the job. Instead, Carpenter became involved with the lower-profile King adaptation *Christine*, a job he took on purely for the money.

Christine (1983)

Directed by: John Carpenter
Produced by: Richard Kobritz
Written by: Bill Phillips
Music: Alan Howarth and John Carpenter
Cast: Keith Gordon (Arnie), Harry Dean Stanton (Junkins), John Stockwell (Dennis), Alexandra Paul (Leigh), Robert Prosky (Garage Owner)
110mins

Arnie Cunningham is a bit of a geek. In fact, he's a lot of a geek, complete with zero babe-pulling power and a set of Buddy Holly spectacles. Still, the specs should help when Arnie falls in love with an older woman who really digs rock 'n' roll. Her name is Christine and she likes to be treated well. She's got 93,000 miles on the clock and cost him a cool 250 bucks. His best friend Dennis warns him it's 'a piece of shit', his parents are furious, and he ends up having to rent Christine a place at Darnell's dingy garage. 'For the first time in my life,' he says, 'I've found something uglier than me... and I can fix her up.' What Arnie doesn't know is that Christine is bad to the bone, a killer car that had injured one man and killed another before she was even off the production line. She demands dedication from her partners; indeed, Christine caused the death of her previous owner's wife and daughter before he himself ended up sucking on the exhaust. Arnie is treating her right, though, doing her up to look just like she did in 1957. Even her clock is running backwards. And the radio? Hey, it's just rock 'n' roll 'n' rock 'n' roll, baby. Arnie's looking better too; he's ditched the glasses and likes nothing better than to cruise in his girl. Sure, he still has problems with Buddy's gang, but his confidence begins to improve. He even gets himself a non-metallic girlfriend in the shape of Leigh. However, disaster strikes when Buddy and his boys think it'd be a real wheeze if they trashed Christine and dumped on her dashboard. It doesn't take long for the gang to regret their actions as they are brutally slain by the relentless motor. Detective Rudolph Junkins has to solve the string of deaths but the clues are illogical – if the car is the killer, then why is Christine so pristine?

Christine may lack any form of message or deep subtext, but at least it's got rock 'n' roll. There's no doubt about it – the car's the star. It is crucial to the credibility of the film that Christine has as much personality as any of the human characters. Right from the opening she stands out, the one crimson car in a line of drab vehicles, with such a vibrant colour scheme complete with polished chrome that you know she's bad. To reflect her time, the radio is constantly tuned to rock 'n' roll music but the songs are chosen by Christine to reflect her mood or impart information. In this way, she has three voices: her engine sounds that indicate pleasure or anger, her radio, and her 'body language', which usually results in death and mayhem. The radio is her chief means of communication, killing to Buddy Holly's *Not Fade Away* or refusing Dennis entry to the strains of *You Keep on Knocking but You Can't Come In*.

Arnie is destined to drive Christine. She uses sexual persuasion to lure desperate men and Arnie is most definitely desperate – 'I need a girl to get laid.' Christine is that girl. Any doubts about car/girl/penis envy are quickly dispelled by the current owner, who informs the boys that the car has 'the finest smell in the world, except for pussy', knowing full well that, for Arnie, desire has no price. Arnie is the typical Stephen King geek boy, a weakling schmuck with zero charisma who is fortunate that he doesn't live near a beach – otherwise he'd constantly be brushing off the sand that was kicked into his face. How much better does he feel when he has a big car, a sexy girlfriend and the ability not just to stand up to the bullies, but to invoke death by proxy? But there lies the rub. He has no control over his life. The qualities that inexplicably led hunky Dennis to be his best friend have vanished, leaving an explosive, rude, self-centred narcissist. Given these central characters and the high-school setting, Carpenter has little to hang the characterisation on – Dennis is too good to be true, Leigh is underdeveloped and Arnie is either a puerile geek or an aggressive psychotic. This costs the film its edge. In the novel, King had 600 pages to create some sympathy for Arnie, Dennis and Leigh, but, when reduced to a film narrative, the luxury of extended characterisation is the first thing to go. This is not to say *Christine* is a bad film; it's one of the better King adaptations. It's just lacklustre when compared with Carpenter's other work.

Things start rolling when the dream begins to turn sour and Buddy's gang smash Christine. It is the first time that the film uses distinctive Carpenter music to denote the impending violation of Arnie's girl. The first major spate of killings – those of Buddy's gang – are classic Carpenter. The camera prowls around Christine as she stalks her first incredulous victim. Blam! Christine's lights bedazzle with such intensity that the lens flare takes up most of the screen. Even without the increasingly persistent score, you know this guy's days are numbered. He runs down the alleyway (always a good place to meet your maker in a Carpenter film) and is squished as Christine scrapes her way towards him. The following night's action is even more explosive as the rest of the gang get the Christine treatment. After goading her, they panic and drive to a petrol station. She wrecks their car and causes the station to go up in flames. Buddy? He's hot-footing it down the highway. Behind him, bursting from the flames like a demon from Hell, is Christine, a fiery avenger with headlight eyes leaving a trail of ignited debris in her wake. The rest of the film never manages to sustain the intensity and style of these scenes. The showdown is marred by its blandness – the restoration of order and the punishment of transgressors. Moral: know your place; only good lookers succeed; respect authority.

Producer Richard Kobritz had previously worked with Carpenter on *Someone's Watching Me!* as well as Tobe Hooper's version of King's *Salem's Lot* (1979) and had amassed a sizeable budget of $10 million. Over $500,000 was spent on the twenty-three 1958 Plymouth Fury cars that were used in the production. The scenes of Christine's reconstructions are wonderfully executed, especially considering they are pre-CGI, with crumpled, scratched metal unfolding into shining red paintwork and gleaming chrome.

Christine is eminently watchable, enjoyable horror fun that does exactly what a good Hollywood no-brainer should. Its weakness lies in the necessarily sketchy characterisation and an unsatisfactory conclusion.

Carpenter's next project had a troubled history. *Starman* was a romantic science-fiction adventure which had many similarities with *ET*. However, in the light of the latter's success, Columbia pictures were keen to ensure that this production had the right approach. This was in part due to the fact that the studio had actually turned down *ET* some years before. Various directors and writers had become involved with *Starman* but nothing had taken off, although executive producer Michael Douglas was very keen that the picture should be made. Carpenter was interested in the concept of an alien discovering humanity while Douglas's confidence in his ability to tell an emotional story whilst not compromising the action led to him being signed up.

Starman (1984)

Directed by: John Carpenter
Produced by: Larry J Franco
Written by: Bruce A Evans, Raynold Gideon
Cast: Jeff Bridges (Starman), Karen Allen (Jenny Hayden), Charles Martin Smith (Mark Shermin), Richard Jaeckel (George Fox), Robert Phalen (Major Bell)
110 mins

'Do you seriously expect me to tell the president that an alien has landed, assumed the identity of a dead housepainter from Madison, Wisconsin, and is presently out tooling around the countryside in a hopped up orange and black 1977 Mustang?'

He may be an extra-terrestrial but he's got balls. He is Starman, visitor from a distant world. Voyager 2's 'medley of musical compositions' and request to 'please visit planet Earth' has paid dividends, encouraging intergalactic tourism and he is first to arrive. The landing is bumpy but fortunately he comes across a place to stay at the house of Jenny Hayden. Jenny's having a tough time of it as her beloved husband Scott has died recently. Naturally she is unimpressed with a visitation, especially one that manifests itself on her living-room floor and proceeds to grow from embryo to adult in front of her eyes. What's more, it looks just like her dear dead Scott. But Starman has his own problems. He needs to reach the rest of his touring party in three days or they'll leave without him, a situation that would see him stranded on alien soil and result in his death. Unfortunately, the rendezvous point is in 'Arizona Maybe', a long way to go if your spaceship is bust, so he coerces Jenny into driving him there, effectively kidnapping her. Slowly she begins to realise that he is not dangerous, just confused and desperate. On top of the long journey and tight deadline, they have one more obstacle to overcome – the government. NASA's hippies may well have sent an interplanetary invite for a party on Earth, but the authorities are determined to poop out big time and wreck the festivities. Finding Starman's abandoned space pod, they set off in hot pursuit. Meanwhile, Starman reveals the source of some pretty impressive powers: his balls. These innocuous little marble-like objects allow him to do anything from resurrecting dead deer to devastating acres of forest, but he only has a limited number. His finest asset, though, is his heart, which gives him the power to perform the greatest miracle of them all...

Soppy romance films – the heartache of love and loss, the outcome causing tears if good, tears if bad, tears if both. How could the genre formula of boy meets girl, boy loses girl, boy (maybe) gets girl become more appealing to an audience who prefer their films a bit more, well, lively? The normal solution is to place it amidst a backdrop of conflict or social upheaval: the *Gone with the Wind* (1939) or *Dr Zhivago* (1965) approach. Another, more radical, solution would be to make the boy a totally different species, bung in some spaceships, a big chase, guns, military helicopters and blow away half the American landscape. Enter Starman. *Starman* is like *ET* (he even has the glowing finger that starts cars) but better and without those awful kids; the film is sentimental and saccharine but filled with enough genuine 'niceness' to be endearing.

In many respects, *Starman* shares its basic premise with *The Thing* in that an alien crash lands to Earth and assumes human form. The difference is that Starman is basically a nice guy and not a ruthless killer, but has the ability to be just as violent should the situation require it. His goodness is fragile; we have no idea of an alien's concept of morality or behaviour. Indeed, he has to ask Jenny to 'define love', not just from the perspective of linguistics but also conceptually. *Starman* is less concerned with examining alien cultures than it is about using alien eyes to interpret the human condition. Starman himself is a springboard from which we can understand the beauty of love and the cruelty of persecution. If we send a message of peace to the universe, why do we attack the first response? The authorities react as though any alien life form would want to conquer the world; from their viewpoint, any other reason for a visit is unthinkable. As in *The Day the Earth Stood Still* (1951), they shoot first and ask questions later. The exception is Mark Shermin, the decent side of government. A scientist working for SETI, he is sympathetic to the concept of a peaceful alien and is quick to point out that presumption of violent intent is not only misguided but also unfair, as 'we invited him here'. His reward for being pragmatic and genuinely interested is that he fulfils his dream – he gets to talk, albeit briefly, to an extra-terrestrial. This convinces him to allow Starman to escape; he is selfless enough not to allow an innocent to be destroyed by ignorant militarism.

Oscar-nominated Jeff Bridges as a loveable alien certainly has an otherworldly air about him, although some of his shaky mannerisms appear slightly similar to the Thermians from *Galaxy Quest* (1999). What does work is his slow progression to developing human characteristics despite the fact he points out that he isn't Jenny's husband Scott on a number of occasions – 'I look like Scott so you be not... little bit jumpy.' While he has an impressive knowledge of languages, he has no context for using them; there is no application. His vocabulary is limited to the words broadcast by the Voyager, so he needs to acquire a wider context for his speech in order to communicate properly. Rather like Kim Novak in *Vertigo* (1958) he is given an identity to 'become'; he may look like Scott all the way through, but essentially he assimilates 'Scott-ness'. This progresses further through Jenny's coaching into language and behaviour; he 'becomes' Scott because she has programmed him to be so. While he admits that he comes from a beautiful planet that is free from war, there is a sense that he respects the human race for daring to be individuals. When he returns to his home world he will be a rarity because he has contracted the 'disease' of humanity – an individual in a society of virtual clones. Individuality can lead to violence and militarism but can also give us the propensity for love and compassion.

Starman's ace card lies in the contrast between big and small, one man against an army. Central to the film is the relationship between Starman and Jenny. It is about as small-scale as you can get – two people (for want of a better term) falling in love but being forced apart due to circumstances they cannot control. Against this is the backdrop of spectacle writ large across the screen;

it's a romance played out between the stars, so the expanse of space, the chasm between worlds, needs to contrast with the microcosmic tale. The film opens beyond the Earth with the Voyager 2 space module drifting through the rings of Saturn. When Starman's ship crashes it rips through the American countryside, scorching a huge swathe of trees. The final showdown sees Starman fleeing to his mother ship with half the US Army in hot pursuit; despite Starman's avowed pacifism, they are going in hard, guns and bombs blazing. This is a wonderfully realised effects sequence taking full advantage of both technology and the epic feel of a wide screen. The mother ship is absolutely huge, a mirrored, gleaming example of alien technology with its surface reflecting the military helicopters that are bombing it. Despite the wonder that accompanies this impressive display the overall feeling remains, if you'll forgive the pun, down to Earth.

While not likely to appeal to the audience who screamed at *Halloween* or grossed-out to *The Thing*, *Starman* still manages to be a Carpenter film. One for dewy-eyed romantics who don't mind saccharine sentimentalities and occasionally ludicrous plot elements, it is also one of the few Carpenter films that features a sex scene – and it has a PG rating! A TV series based on *Starman* was launched in 1986 and ran for one season.

Starman was a hit and gave Carpenter much-needed confidence after the disastrous reception of *The Thing*. A couple of scripts he'd written were picked up by the studios and he became executive producer on both *The Philadelphia Experiment* and *Black Moon Rising*. Although neither film was directed by Carpenter, both films were successful and his name on the credits certainly did them no harm. Also around this time, his son, John Cody, was born. His next directing role was to encompass his love for Hong Kong movies, and although he was actually offered the chance to direct Eddie Murphy in *The Golden Child* (1986), he turned it down in favour of something big...

Big Trouble in Little China (1986)

Directed by: John Carpenter
Produced by: Larry Franco
Written by: Gary Goldman and David Z Weinstein
Director of Photography: Dean Cundey
Music: John Carpenter and Alan Howarth
Cast: Kurt Russell (Jack Burton), Dennis Dun (Wang Chi), Victor Wong (Egg Shen), Kim Cattrall (Gracie Law), James Hong (Lo Pan), Suzee Pai (Miao Yin)
96 mins

> *'Do you believe in sorcery?'*
> *'Of course... because it's real.'*

Jack Burton is soon to find out that Chinese culture is not limited to all-night gambling with his friend Wang from whom he has just won a doubled-up bet. He accompanies Wang to the airport to pick up bride-to-be Miao Yin, straight from Peking, but unfortunately straight into the hands of a group of hoodlums with superior martial arts skills. What distinguishes Miao Yin is that she has green eyes, highly prized and very rare. So rare that Lo Pan, a sprightly 2,000-year-old sorcerer, needs her for a ceremony to restore his youth and virility. Now Lo Pan really isn't a nice chap and keeps appalling company in the shape of a gang of hard-hitting, fast-shooting, weapon-wielding thugs and the Three Storms, a motley band of supernatural warriors with wide-brimmed straw hats. Jack hits Lo Pan with his truck, the Pork Chop Express, and is perturbed to find that it has no effect. 'Comes out of thin air in the middle of a goddamned alley... he just stands there waiting for my truck to drive straight through him with light coming out of his mouth!' After a failed rescue attempt at a Chinese brothel and the disappearance of the Pork Chop Express, Jack and Wang team up for an all-out assault on Lo Pan's headquarters. Brave? Yes. Foolhardy? Yes.

Captured? You bet. Beaten up, tied into a pair of wheelchairs and left in a cell, their prospects don't look sunny. Still, they're foolhardy enough to try again, this time with nosy, green-eyed lawyer Gracie Law in tow. But if they're in trouble, what about Miao Yin, captured by the Storms, and Gracie, seized by a scary monster, now also in the hands of the dreaded Lo Pan? They are garbed in red bridal gowns and awaiting a test to see if they can tame the burning blade – a ritual that, if successful, will see Lo Pan resurrected in his youthful flesh, ready to unleash his dark powers on the world...

'I am a reasonable guy but I have seen some very unreasonable things.'

In retrospect, it is easy to see why *Big Trouble in Little China* did such mediocre business upon its original release; it was just too far ahead of its time. The Hong Kong film industry had moved on from those 'you killed my sifu' days of the 1970s and was producing some of the most intense and exciting cinema in the world, but only die-hard cineastes and fanatics could see these in the West. *Big Trouble in Little China* is a Western response to the magical cinema of the East, an introduction to some themes of Hong Kong cinema within a simple, palatable, Western framework. It mixes the macho posturing of the Western hero with elements of Eastern fantasies to produce something the likes of which had not been seen in Hollywood. Although there are numerous elements that look back to the popular 1970s Hong Kong films, as well as the Japanese Baby Cart series, the main point of reference is Tsui Hark's seminal New Wave fantasy *Zu: Warriors from the Magic Mountain* (1983). Zu's dazzling array of quirky and hyperkinetic special effects remains a landmark in Hong Kong cinema, director Hark enlisting the aid of Western special-effects artists to realise an Eastern vision, the results of which are bounced back for integration into *Big Trouble in Little*

China. In terms of more Western influences, Mike Hodges' camp masterpiece *Flash Gordon* (1980) has a lot to answer for in the costume and lighting department as well as Lo Pan's easy comparison with Ming the Merciless.

Key to the film is Jack, our rugged hero. He provides our gateway into another world and his discoveries are ours too. What makes his character so memorable is the conflict between his accepted modes of behaviour and the results of his actions. Normally we expect the macho hero to brave the elements, occasionally fall foul of bad luck or some devious plan, but to come up trumps overall. Not so here, although it must be stressed that Jack is a very brave man. The comedy in the film is derived mainly from the fact that Jack's attempts at chivalry are not only ineffectual, but misguided and potentially dangerous too. Blindly stumbling into any crisis, he is doomed to failure; he has no knowledge of Chinese culture or traditions, despite his affinity with the community. Jack tries to save Miao Yin at the airport. He gets beaten. Jack tries again at the brothel. He gets beaten. At best, he can watch with incredulity as bodies fly hither and thither. His running, diving and general ignorance regarding his own impotence reaches its nadir when he uses that trustworthy penis-extension of every macho Western hero – the gun. Going gung-ho into the enemy's lair waving his gun around he epitomises the heroic male... until he lets off a burst of fire and is knocked out by the resulting falling debris. Linked with this is the macho dialogue. When Wang asks, 'Are you ready Jack?' the response is the inevitable, 'I was born ready.' As the climax approaches, Jack and his band have crossed the sewers to infiltrate the enemy stronghold; at his muted request to 'follow the leader' he whips open the door in front of him, only to face a bunch of hoodlums. He promptly shuts the door on them and admits, 'We may be trapped.' Not that Wang and Jack have the monopoly on cheesy dialogue – Egg is full of cod philosophy and occasionally meaningless advice. But at least he normally knows what to do and uses his strengths to bolster the others' performance with counter magic and nifty bus driving. Jack's final humiliation is also his most triumphant moment. Having confronted Lo Pan, he is quick to catch the blade and kills the evil sorcerer for good. His heroics are marred, however, because he is wearing lipstick, having just kissed Gracie – his final attempt at masculinity thwarted.

What *Big Trouble in Little China* also gains from Hong Kong films are the fight scenes, which are intense, fast and feature lots of grown men throwing each other around. Indeed, one of the Three Storms (Thunder) is played by Carter Wong, a Shaw Brothers veteran of such films as *Fatal Flying Guillotines* (1977) and *Hapkido* (1972), which also featured Jackie Chan and Sammo Hung. In the first major brawl, Carpenter disappoints us initially by having the two gangs pull guns on each other but this is a ruse to make the following fight more exciting. We are shown how much more interesting it is to have 'real' man-to-man combat than the cowardly distancing gunplay. Guns are not creative, they are not respectful and, in *Big Trouble*, generally not much use. Jack is shocked by his own gun use and even the evil Lords of Death get rid of their weapons to make the brawl more personal. The final showdown is as spectacular as any Shaw Brothers classic.

So what if the plot is ludicrous? The pace and sheer *joie de vivre* drag you from one set piece to the next without pausing for breath. The score drives everything along, initially macho guitars to reflect our view of Jack (as the *Escape from New York* hero with bared arms and big boots) before settling into a stream of synthesiser riffs. Visually, the camerawork is as fluid as ever but really excels in the gloriously lit finale at the kitsch temple, where idols are surrounded by neon lights and there's always glitter in the air. For one of the first times in a Western film wirework is used stylistically and extensively. By having the actors strung on very fine wire that is imperceptible on film, it is possible to convey superhuman strength and power. Wirework has since become popular with such films as *The Matrix* (1999) and is now an accepted part of the Hollywood aesthetic arsenal. Wirework conveys the choreographed ballet of martial arts fighting so much more poetically.

The tagline gives it away – 'A Mystical, Action, Adventure, Comedy, Kung Fu, Monster, Ghost Story!' You almost feel they should've put a musical number in just to round everything off. There's a big ruck at the airport. An ugly Yeti-type monster that appears from nowhere and terrorises the cast. Eyes appear *Scooby Doo*-style behind pictures. Lightning flies from hands. There are pitched gunfights. There are pitched fistfights. There's a hysterical panic in a brothel. Magical rays are emitted from eyes and mouths. Magic weapons. A six-demon bag. Fighting deities. Dodgy coppers. What more do you want? It's a film ripe for rediscovery – big, loud fun in the tradition of Saturday morning serials but with that crucial Eastern twist. Analysts can watch it as a deconstruction of the male ego in the climate of the Reagan/Thatcher era, or the castration of the hero figure, but in the final tally *Big Trouble in Little China* is unadulterated fun from start to finish.

Unfortunately, the film's disappointing returns meant that a sequel was written but never made. The prospects of a TV spin-off also fell by the wayside, although interest in the film has increased over the years.

BACK TO BASICS

Big Trouble bombed. Western audiences were simply not ready for such a revolutionary film and even the critics hated it. Carpenter was hugely disappointed and decided to leave the studio system and return to independent, smaller productions where he could have more control. He signed a four-picture deal with Alive Films who gave him that all-important freedom.

Prince of Darkness (1987)

Directed by: John Carpenter
Produced by: Larry Franco
Written by: Martin Quatermass (guess who?)
Director of Photography: Gary Kibbe
Music: Alan Howarth and John Carpenter
Cast: Donald Pleasence (Priest), Lisa Blount (Catherine), Victor Wong (Prof Birack), Jameson Parker (Brian), Susan Blanchard (Kelly), Ann Howard (Susan), Dennis Dun (Walter)
101 mins

'In fact, YOU WILL NOT BE SAVED.'

For nearly 2,000 years the Brotherhood of Sleep have kept it hidden from the world. Now the keeper of the key, Father Carlton, is dead and the secret can be kept no more because the sleeper awakens. Deep in the bowels of an unassuming church lies an ancient artefact, a swirling, pulsating green liquid contained in an ornate flask. Ideas about its origins and meaning have been recorded in a huge ledger. The new keeper, Priest, instantly recognises that it is stirring, that religious denial is no longer appropriate and that scientific, philosophical and theological opinion is required.

Professor Birack enlists some of his more eclectic students, with the promise of extra credit, for a weekend of study at the church. He is initially sceptical of religious dogma and prefers to rely on quantum theories of uncertainty and non-linear time; as he puts it, 'our logic collapses on the subatomic level into ghosts and shadows.' However, there is no doubt that something is decidedly odd about the artefact – it carbon dates at seven million years and can only be opened from the inside. Meanwhile, outside the church, the local hobo community are congregating, the sun and moon are looking decidedly strange and the insect population seems to be mustering with some unknown purpose. The team begin to understand that they are dealing with a powerful alien consciousness, older than the human race, which seeks to walk the Earth once more. Susan is assaulted by the spraying liquid that spouts from the artefact into her mouth and she becomes possessed. Susan finds further disciples, willing or unwilling, the evil spreading like contagion amongst the group. The remaining conscious humans can't escape because the building has been blockaded and they are under constant attack from their former colleagues. Lisa and Susan, ghosts of their former selves, arrange the artefact to raise the long-captive beast into human form using Kelly as a host. Kelly rises as the Prince of Darkness, seeking to release her father who was trapped millions of years ago.

Right from the very opening, *Prince of Darkness* seeks to be an intense film with an increasing sense of foreboding. While many of Carpenter's more popular films have relied upon a single focused goal, made clear to the audience early on in proceedings, *Prince of Darkness* is more concerned with sustaining its narrative drive throughout the entire running time. The second part in Carpenter's Apocalypse Trilogy, it offers little room for emotional introspection amidst the mustering forces of evil. The horror is derived from the characters' situation rather than significant emotional attachment to them because we are dealing with a group effort to uncover the mystery rather than the singular actions of a clearly defined protagonist. Not only are the group trapped inside the building, under siege from a faceless horde, there are evils inside to contend with as well. The myriad of threats and the variety of characters we are meant to identify with allows questions of the nature of humanity, religion and the origins of the species to be argued without focusing on one overriding individual or ideal. Birack's concepts of subatomic particles do not actually conflict with Priest's visions of deity but complement them. There's an indication that man needs to have attained a certain level of scientific knowledge to comprehend what is happening and the church's teachings are merely an earlier attempt at understanding an alien culture.

Despite the scientific overtones the film is predominantly signposted as horror. There are plenty of grotesque and surreal moments of the macabre to pique casual interest and numerous asides to other horror films. The accelerated pregnancy was pre-empted in Donald Cammels' *Demon Seed* (1977) and would later resurface in Carpenter's Masters of Horror *Pro-life* episode. When the group rescue Walter from the cupboard as he watches the metamorphosis, the influence is pure Romero. When Wyndham is first killed he finds himself covered in cockroaches and a tramp stabs him repeatedly in a scene similar to one in Argento's surrealist shocker *Inferno* (1978). As in Argento's films (notably *Profondo Rosso* [1975] and *Phenomena* [1985], which also starred Donald Pleasence), insects play a big role, both in concepts of telepathy and as harbingers of misfortune. Like the Prince of Darkness, they have inhabited Earth for longer than humankind; they are his brethren. The window pane strains to ever increasing numbers of worms, rotten meat is filled with maggots, the tramps have insects on their faces and our first glimpse of Professor Birack is accompanied in long shot, craning down to an extreme close-up of red ants. When the liquid strikes it is a perversion of the sacrament – a spurt sprayed into the mouth of the victim. When passed on from mouth to mouth it is like the transmission of the aphrodisiac-venereal-disease parasite from David Cronenberg's *Shivers* (1975).

If there is a weakness in the film it lies in the very epic (although microcosmic) scale of the events which overwhelm the characters and to some extent alienate the audience. This is community characterisation at its best; you cannot anticipate who will survive because they all have personalities that can be admired, but all have faults too. Priest is decent enough to realise that he needs help but ineffectual when he gets it; the Professor is intelligent and reasoned but blinkered in his dogma; Catherine's an enigma; Brian's just not credible; and Walter's a nice guy, but trite. This makes the film more believable, but also renders it as chaotic as the ideas it espouses – it destabilises audience identification with a core group. You are left with a struggle between good and evil on a large scale where the hope of humanity lies beyond the concerns of the individual. *Prince of Darkness* allows these paradoxes to be aired in the context of a gross horror film. The whole film is one long mood builder with one of Carpenter's most downbeat scores driving events forward with increasing momentum. While certain sections of the score hark back to earlier pieces (notably *Assault on Precinct 13*, which also bears structural similarities) the effect is more to drive the earnestness of the revelations or signpost new atrocities rather than creating a soundscape for action.

Prince of Darkness's special effects are imaginative rather than expensive and can still hold their own because of this. The creepy shots of green liquid oozing from the capsule and dripping upward look strangely surreal but are no more than an upside-down camera, some careful editing and ever reliable lighting from cinematographer Gary Kibbe. Similarly, the organic flows of the conscious liquid are achieved by simple film reversal. The effects are reminiscent of Jean Cocteau's surrealist masterpiece *Le Sang d'un poète* (1930), particularly in the climactic scenes showing the attempts of an assimilated Kelly to rescue her trapped 'father' from the abyss beyond the mirror. Careful use of camera angles and reflections allow the actress to move through the mirror as through a pool. The counter-shots of an alien hand reaching out for freedom are menacingly evocative. The final shots of Catherine's despair as she reaches out to return to the world following her self-sacrifice are haunting in their simplicity.

In terms of narrative *Prince of Darkness* owes a great debt to the works of Nigel Kneale, particularly *Quatermass and the Pit* in which a mysterious artefact is discovered in London and throws into doubt the origin of humankind. This should give some indication that *Prince of Darkness*'s writer, Martin Quatermass, is in fact Carpenter himself. He has taken the principles of Kneale's use of cutting-edge scientific theory to drive a genre narrative and brought it up to date, precisely what Kneale was doing between the 1950s and 1970s. Although *Prince of Darkness* is flawed, it is, nevertheless, a brave stab at cerebral horror.

They Live (1988)

Directed by: John Carpenter
Produced by: Larry Franco
Associate Producer: Sandy King
Written by: Frank Armitage
Director of Photography: Gary Kibbe
Music: John Carpenter and Alan Howarth
Cast: 'Rowdy' Roddy Piper (Nada), Keith David (Frank), Meg Foster (Holly), George 'Buck' Flower (Drifter)
95 mins

'Keep us asleep, keep us selfish, keep us sedated.'

Nada is a drifter, forced on the road because he has been made redundant from his job of ten years. He is not alone; the rich are getting richer and the poor poorer, and finding work ain't easy. Still, he's persistent and he gains employment on a construction site. There he meets Frank who takes him to a shantytown for the destitute, where food is handed out to the needy but families can still watch TV. Central to the community is the church, overseen by the blind hellfire-and-brimstone Reverend, but Nada discovers that the whole thing is a front for a bizarre underground organisation. What has this to do with the hacked broadcasts that occasionally mar the bland, incessant whine of consumerist TVs? After the police raid the church, Nada manages to recover one of the organisation's boxes. It doesn't contain guns or drugs. It's full of sunglasses. When he puts a pair on their Hoffman lenses allow him to see the world as it really is. Signs, magazines, even tins of peaches all preach messages to pacify and make the consumer conform. Obey. Sleep. Submit. Consume. Marry and reproduce. Do not question authority. Even more disturbing is that some of the everyday people he bumps into aren't people at all, but 'formaldehyde-face' alien humanoids with revolting skin, while the city streets are patrolled by 'invisible' floating cameras. Unfortunately, his attitude means that the aliens become aware that he can see them and he is forced on the run. He kidnaps passer-by Holly to escape his pursuers; she takes him to her house but manages to chuck him out of her window when his guard is down. He must cónvince the world that they are under alien threat, but if he can't even get through to Frank what hope is there? With the aliens pumping out messages of conformity and humans colluding with them, he needs to join an underground resistance movement to arouse the masses against their bourgeois extra-terrestrial oppressors. And to make matters worse, he's all out of bubblegum.

They Live is not a wrestling movie but it does feature one of the then WWF's biggest stars, the bagpipe-playing, kilted crowd-pleaser 'Rowdy' Roddy Piper, and contains one of the longest one-on-one fights in (American, at least) screen history. At over five minutes long, the punch-up between Frank and Nada is a complete scream. Nada is trying to get Frank to see the real world – 'put on these glasses or start eating that trash can' – but Frank is having none of it. They slug it out until they are both bloody pulps. The sheer length of the scene turns it from that of character conflict to comedy. This is not Nada's first fight of the film – he has already taken out a policeman using that popular wrestling manoeuvre 'The Clothesline' before lapsing into more 'normal' film fighting techniques. If this makes proceedings sound trite or cartoonish it is because the film manages to be both a serious critique of capitalist consumer mores and a feel-good exploitation action flick, in roughly equal proportions. The Carpenter male has progressed from the earlier Hawks-based template into something altogether more appropriate to attitudes of the age; the macho man is dead – long live the new action hero. Nada's role in the film is an extension of Kurt Russell's character in *Big Trouble in Little China*. He's not as ineffectual but shares the same ability to blurt out total rubbish in the name of machismo – a parody of the prevalent contemporary hero. When Nada spouts such eminently repeatable dialogue as 'I have come here to chew bubblegum and kick ass, and I'm all out of bubblegum' (as appropriated for the computer game *Duke Nukem 3D*) or 'Life's a bitch and she's back in heat' we laugh at him, not with him. He represents the dream gone sour, his awakening a response to the repressive conservative Reagan/Thatcher policies that crippled creativity in the 1980s. Like so many others, he has been asleep and just accepted his fate. In his own words: 'I believe in America. I follow the rules' – but only when the rules are transparent and fair. When the system is shown to be corrupt, he ignites. All the public wants is to be like the beautiful people they see on television. They don't know the truth but, importantly, they don't care. Thematically, the film is very much in the Philip K Dick mould (despite being based on a story by Ray Faraday Nelson) in that the central character finds that his perception of reality does not truly represent the world around him. Only when he dons the special glasses does he see the world as it is, but this gives him a massive headache both literally and conceptually.

When Frank and Nada track down the resistance, their attempts to join the urban guerrilla network are suppressed when their den is raided, but our heroes escape to an alleyway. The subsequent gunplay unwinds like the opening of *Assault on Precinct 13* although the luxury of smoother tracking has allowed the camera to penetrate or retreat down the alleyway to accentuate the dynamism of proceedings. The harsh red-and-green lighting gives the scene an almost comic-book feel which neatly pushes the film from dystopian nightmare into the realms of more traditional Hollywood science-fiction films – we've had our message, now we can get on with the action. Escaping the alleyway by conveniently opening a portal brings the narrative into more conventional science-fiction action with bizarre teleportations via departure Alpha-7 to Andromeda, alien-human dinner parties, Cable 54 broadcasts and plenty of machine-gun antics. Of course, you know that, in the end, the alien invasion is going to be revealed to a stunned populace, but there are still some twists and a defiant middle finger to come from Nada prior to his long journey to the stars.

The fact that the sunglasses allow Nada to view the real world both reinforces the perception of the 80s action hero and provides the film with much of its visual drive – the ordinary as extraordinary. Rather like Jean-Luc Godard's *Alphaville* (1965), *They Live* constructs most of its futuristic elements from contemporary or older items – the cars were dated in 1988, the teleporters and communication devices are simply wristwatches, even the sounds of the choir are recorded on a reel-to-reel tape machine. In this sense the film has dated little – it was anachronistic at the time. This means the limitations of the budget actually work in the film's favour. The result of putting on the glasses is a simple visual motif, a change from colour to black-and-white film stock, reminiscent of Tarkovsky's *Stalker* (1979) or Powell and Pressberger's *A Matter of Life and Death* (1946). Accompanying the downbeat situation is a suitably bluesy score that rattles like the passing train that opens the film. A slight departure from a normal Carpenter soundtrack, this looks forward to the more guitar-based music which will also be heard in *Vampires* and *Ghosts of Mars*. Aside from Nada's nihilistic designation, most characters are defined by their attributes rather than being given arbitrary names (e.g. Family Man's Daughter, Biker, Blonde Haired Cop, Ingénue, Well-Dressed Customer), which is very much in keeping with the tone of the film. *They Live* was based on a short story called *Eight O'Clock in the Morning* by Ray Faraday Nelson and Carpenter adapted it for the screen using the pseudonym Frank Armitage. As an exploitation film criticising the consumerist American society that paradoxically allowed it to be made, *They Live* shares values with another great, cheap, American independent horror film – George A Romero's *Dawn of the Dead* (1978). It comes as no surprise to find that, at the end of the film, when the populace at large can see the aliens on television, a film critic derides the horror film by stating, 'Filmmakers such as George Romero and John Carpenter have to show some restraint.'

They Live is a blend of socially conscious politics, science fiction, action and comedy which marks it as one of the more unusual and entertaining low-budget films of the 1980s.

'HE WHO HAS THE GOLD MAKES THE RULES'

After *They Live*, Carpenter had a break from directing, and during this time he and Adrienne Barbeau were divorced. A couple of his scripts became TV westerns (*El Diablo* and *Blood River*). He was remarried in 1990, to producer Sandy King, who had already worked with him on several projects and was to become involved with many more. Both *Prince of Darkness* and *They Live* had been successful, which gave Carpenter the confidence to return to the major studios for another bash at big-budget productions. He was to become involved with Chevy Chase on *Memoirs of an Invisible Man*. Chase was a huge star at the time and renowned for slapstick and comedy, but on this occasion wanted to prove to the world that he was also a serious actor. Having directed a number of fairly downbeat pictures during the 1980s, this was an opportunity for Carpenter to lighten up.

Memoirs of an Invisible Man (1992)

Directed by: John Carpenter
Produced by: Bruce Bodner and Dan Kulsrud
Written by: Robert Collector, Dana Olsen and William Goldman from the book by HF Saint
Music: Shirley Walker
Cast: Chevy Chase (Nick Halloway), Daryl Hannah (Alice Monroe),

Sam Neill (Jenkins), Michael McKean (George), Stephen Tobolowski (Warren Singleton), Jim Norton (Dr Wachs)
100 mins

'I'm not sick. I'm not crazy, but I am invisible.'

Nick Halloway is a rich and successful lawyer but his life is empty. One night his friend George introduces him to Alice, a beautiful and articulate maker of cosmological and anthropological documentaries. He's so smitten that, when she leaves, he gets blind drunk and turns up to a devastatingly dull lecture the next day with the mother of all hangovers. Trying to find somewhere to sleep, he unwittingly sets off an explosive sequence of events culminating in the evacuation of the Magnoscopics Institute. When he wakes up, he finds that parts of the building have become invisible, a strange affliction which seems to have affected him too. Quick to the scene is David Jenkins, a ruthless government operative who sees the potential for an invisible man in espionage work and is determined to track Nick down as a recruit: 'Assassination is entirely ethical if you're on the right side.' But Nick has other plans. Being invisible is not all about free seats at the cinema and sneaking into girls' changing rooms; just avoiding people is trouble enough and hailing a cab even more of a nightmare than usual. Dr Wachs, who ran the research project, cannot find the cause of the invisibility, so Nick seeks refuge in George's summerhouse. But when George arrives unexpectedly with his wife Ellen, Alice and the amorous and somewhat smarmy Richard, Nick realises that he can't live without the woman he's briefly loved. He reveals his predicament to Alice, unaware that Jenkins and his hardware-enhanced SWAT team have tracked him down...

Memoirs of an Invisible Man features many of the themes that are prevalent in Carpenter's other works, particularly in regard to the lone protagonist facing the might of his own government whose interests are all concerned with self-preservation as opposed to the rights of the citizen. There are Hitchcockian elements too, such as the man-on-the-run plot structure. Like Roger Thornhill in *North By Northwest* (indeed, one of the projects Nick is working on is the Kaplan Project, a reference to that film's MacGuffin), Nick is a corporate nobody forced into a preposterous situation. Carpenter provides self-references, finely realised set pieces, dry humour and even some anti-establishment dialogue – 'Do you expect me to trust a politician?' In the cold light of day it is an enjoyable, big-budget, Hollywood popcorn film, but therein lies the rub. It is like Carpenter squash, diluted so much that there's enough hint to get the flavour, but too insipid to make it wholly satisfactory.

Turning a wry, insular story into a Chevy Chase comedy-romance was never going to be easy and the strains clearly show in the finished piece. When Chase asks the whereabouts of the men's room, he inadvertently causes a scientist to spill coffee on his computer, setting off a chain reaction which culminates in the loss of half the building and resulting in Nick's invisibility. It is a funny scene because it is ludicrous and plot driven, tells us about Nick's attitude and furthers the narrative. Later, Nick has problems getting around town and uses a drunk to hail a cab by knocking him unconscious and treating him like a human mannequin. The concept is darkly funny – after all, Nick had been this intoxicated the previous night. Chase milks this scene for all it's worth, getting the drunk to 'talk' to the driver by moving his lips with his hands, culminating in him faking the man vomiting out of the cab door. A scene with witty potential becomes less interesting and more irritating as it progresses. His later capture at the hands of the evil governmental operative Jenkins makes the humour incongruous. Unfortunately, the whole piece ping-pongs between these extremes; for every moment of grim, sub-Raymond Chandler voiceover about the futility of flight and the inevitability of capture, the pain of not being seen and the anguish of being denied your love, there is a counterpoint of base tomfoolery.

Key to any romance is that the romance must seem right or, at the very least, plausible. Nick is a lecherous businessman. When he first meets the intelligent and charming Alice over dinner, she is reduced to a simpering devoted admirer, slobbering in the ladies' toilets and arranging their next dinner date. She does try to disarm his one-track mind, though; when he glibly states 'Love blonde hair' she responds 'Love garlic'. After this fleeting encounter it is some time before he sees her again, at George's summerhouse being molested by a desperate Richard. Of course, he uses his invisibility to turf Richard out, but stays in the room watching as Alice prepares to go to bed. This seedy side to his nature is fobbed off as love, but basically he is exploiting his position. Indeed, when she questions whether he was in her room that night he initially denies it before confessing, turning his voyeurism into a joke by telling her that he covered his eyes. Of course, he can see through his hands. Alice does help Nick to come to terms with his invisibility, painting a pasty face on him so they can go out to dinner – 'If I had eyes and teeth I'd be a whole head' – and coping with his melancholic outbursts. But the relationship still feels implausible.

Invisible men films have always relied on special effects to carry their credibility. The finest example remains James Whale's visual tour de force *The Invisible Man* (1933) starring Claude Rains. Up until *Memoirs of an Invisible Man* an astonishing 60 years later, the groundbreaking effects work had not been bettered. Carpenter acknowledges Whale's classic in the scene where Nick finally reveals to Alice that he is invisible. Perhaps in an attempt to make her understand more easily, she finds him dressed as Claude Rains, complete with bandaged head, dark glasses and lounge wear, peeling off the bandages to reveal nothing. This scene also reinforces one element that emphasises the extent to which a 'star' must be seen in a film. In Whale's original, and even in Paul Verhoeven's *Hollow Man* (2000), the invisible person remains invisible to the viewer. However, Chase is the star, so we are put in the position of being able to see the unseeable, which, while making the events easier to interpret, interrupts narrative causality. It's far more interesting for the viewer when he cannot be seen, for then ILM (Industrial Light and Magic) can take over. The complexity of the revolutionary effects ranges from elementary visual tricks to intricate and time-consuming CGI. Among the simpler effects is the moment when Nick escapes from Jenkins' office by placing a gun to his head. A combination of Sam Neill's excellent body contortions and a model gun literally stuck to his head make the scene feel surprisingly realistic. At the other end of the scale, Nick has approached Dr Wachs in the park disguised as a tramp in order to get him to find an invisibility cure. But Jenkins' men spot him and Nick flees the park. Running along the streets, he takes off his clothes piece by piece to reveal the emptiness beneath. In the end there is just a pair of trousers running down the road. The sequence is long, exciting and accompanied by a big, loud Hollywood orchestra – escapist entertainment at its best but painstaking to realise. A combination of blue screen, motion tracking and digital painting were used alongside careful model work and in-camera effects to create the shot. While this is all cutting edge, the principle is not far from Whale's original, where the back of the coat's collar hidden by Rains (who was wearing all black) was hand painted frame by frame to complete the illusion. The other way that we 'see' Nick is by reactions to his body. Physically, this manifests itself as objects falling over, doors opening or pens waving in the air. More impressive is when things react on and within Nick. At the beginning we see him chewing gum and blowing a bubble; later the contents of his stomach can be seen being digested (yuck!); and when Nick has a cigarette, we see the smoke entering his lungs before being exhaled. In the penultimate reel Nick can be 'seen' in the rain because of the water that surrounds him.

The main language used in Hollywood is fiscal – the more money something costs, the more nervous studio executives become about the resulting film, resulting in filmmaking by a committee of accountants. This generally has the effect of removing creative control from the director. *Memoirs of an Invisible Man* just about manages to be better than your average summer blockbuster, but it could have been so much more.

Memoirs bombed. Yet again, fortune was not on Carpenter's side when it came to big-budget productions. He was despondent and decided to return to television work after a 14-year break. Working for Showtime, he was allowed enough freedom to inject the kind of violence that network-syndicated terrestrial services would have found hard to stomach.

Body Bags (1993)

Directed by: John Carpenter (*The Gas Station*, *Hair*) and Tobe Hooper (*Eye*)
Produced by: Sandy King
Written by: Billy Brown and Dan Angel
Director of Photography: Gary Kibbe
Music: John Carpenter and Jim Lang
Cast: *Links:* John Carpenter (Coroner); *The Gas Station:* Alex Datcher (Anne), Robert Carradine (Bill), Wes Craven (Pasty Faced Man), Sam Raimi (Dead Attendant); *Hair:* Stacy Keach (Richard), David Warner (Dr Lock), Sheena Easton (Megan), Deborah Harry (Nurse); *Eye:* Mark Hamill (Brent), Twiggy (Cathy), Roger Corman (Dr Bregman)
91 mins

'I love stories about our national past-time – violent death.'

Introducing our horrific host – the Coroner – who gives us a whirlwind tour of his favourite corpses and shares the odd tickled rib. His pet hate? Natural causes.

The Gas Station: Anne has landed herself a night job at the local gas station, giving her plenty of time to brush up on her studies between customers. All would be well but, wouldn't you know it, there's a killer on the loose who has already notched up six bodies and is looking to improve on his psychotic qualifications. Still, Bill, the nice chap who worked the early shift, has given her his phone number should things get a bit scary. All too soon it becomes apparent that there are more than just customers who are interested in the gas station. There are gruesome paintings daubed in the men's toilets and a mutilated body in the staff locker. Anne is definitely not alone...

Hair: Richard is suffering from the ravages of age – follicle degeneration. Unwilling to accept his fate like a man, he goes to inordinate lengths to recover his good locks with a bewildering and expensive array of potions, massagers and unsightly concoctions made from lamb foetuses. However, fortune strikes when he signs up for a new treatment courtesy of Dr Lock, a patented protein that can give him any hair he dares to wear. Rather than a subtle approach he chooses the Stallion look – 'Oh yes! Giddy-up!' – and, sure enough, the next day he's turned into a babe-magnet sex-machine with hair down to his knees. Unfortunately, he has also developed a nasty sore throat and slowly realises that his manly mane is not all it seems. These extra-terrestrial tresses of terror, these felonious follicles have a vicious life of their own and, if a solution isn't found soon, Richard could find himself hair today, gone tomorrow...

Eye: Baseball, like many sports, is far easier at a professional level if you are in possession of stereoscopic vision, so having a big chunk of car windscreen rammed into your eyeball is unlikely to improve your home-run potential. Such an automotive disaster has befallen Brent and it seems as though his career is over. But, as luck would have it, a donor eye is available and the transplant is a success. The adopted optic is not all it seems, however, and, rather like pianists tend to receive the severed hands of executed murderers, this has come straight from the state gas chamber. With increasingly painful migraines and disturbing hallucinations of his wife Cathy, dead and bursting from her unhallowed shallow grave, the future looks grim...

Body Bags' roots are manifold – from anthology films such as *Dr Terror's House of Horrors* (1965), *Creepshow* (1982) and *Dead of Night* (1945), via short 'twist in the tale' television shows (*The Twilight Zone*, *Tales of the Unexpected*) to the EC horror/crime comics of the 1950s. All of these have a literary lineage in the works of Edgar Allan Poe, HP Lovecraft and MR James. Perhaps the most obvious precedent for *Body Bags* is that of *Tales from the Crypt*, the most successful of the EC Horror comics. It was also an Amicus film in 1972 and an unexpected cult television hit in the 1990s. This later entry with an atrociously punning host – The Cryptkeeper from the original comics – traditionally links events with nasty gags and a variety of morbid props. *Body Bags* is clearly in this mould: overtly gory, nasty and ultimately harmless, like the campfire stories of *The Fog*, sufficiently removed from logic to be dismissed but close enough to reality to create a chill. *Body Bags*' three segments easily stand out as separate half-hour programmes, introduced by the Coroner, played by Carpenter himself, with some typically excellent make-up courtesy of Rick Baker. This is a hoot from start to finish, the opening screen emblem a pastiche of the MGM lion, but instead of a roar we have John Carpenter wielding a buzzing chainsaw with the Latin motto Sanguis Gratia Artis (blood for the sake of art).

The best of the bunch is undoubtedly *The Gas Station*, an 'urban myth' film which manages to be a ball of tension from the outset, punctuated by sudden jolts and sticky splatter. Like the best of the stalk 'n' slash genre you are almost shouting

Resurrected for revenge as inclement weather brings in *The Fog*.

Violent alien duplication intent on destruction in *The Thing*.

MacReady for action, Kurt Russell attempts to defend against *The Thing*.

Vocal violence from ancient magical enemy Lo Pan in *Big Trouble in Little China*.

Oh brother, where art thou? Laurie Strode (Jamie Lee Curtis) prepares to defend herself from the Shape in *Halloween*.

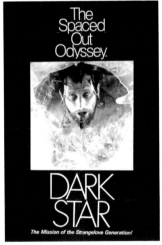

Poster revelations – gang warfare in *Assault on Precinct 13*, car trouble in *Christine*, holiday horror in *Halloween* and spaced out humour in *Dark Star*.

Optical revelation of alien invasion and Nada's all out of bubblegum in *They Live*.

Jenny (Karen Allen) finds that true humanity doesn't require 'Scott' (Jeff Bridges) actually to be human in the romance *Starman*.

Katrina (Sheryl Lee) soon to be assaulted by *John Carpenter's Vampires*.

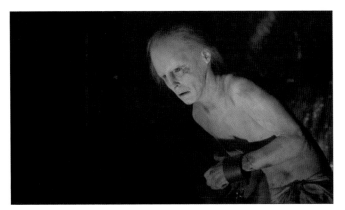

Fallen angel in *Masters of Horror: Cigarette Burns*.

Kristen (Amber Heard), gazing at the smouldering remains of the house she's just burned down, is about to face the never-ending horror of *The Ward*.

Planet of the Snake. Kurt Russell as Snake Plissken seeks *Escape From New York*.

Going, going, gone. Chevy Chase and Daryl Hannah in *Memoirs of an Invisible Man*.

at the screen 'Don't leave the self-locking booth!' or 'He's behind you!' as events escalate. It may be derivative but as a technical exercise in scaring the audience it is a lovely piece of filmmaking. Good, murky camerawork, tight pacing and powerful atmospherics make the most of the necessarily slim storyline and are enhanced by some superb performances and the prerequisite twist at the end.

Hair, in contrast, is a hysterical gross comedy with Stacy Keach going to extreme measures to keep his hair on. At one point his long-suffering girlfriend kisses his head only to end up with a mouthful of the black paint that he's used to cover up his bald patch! Naturally, the alien-brain-cultivators plotline resulting in savage serpentine hair is as preposterous as one can imagine, but this is what makes the piece so enjoyable – it's ludicrous enough to last its running time with Keach hamming it up to the max in his Stallion hairstyle and grabbing at the wiggling snake hairs that are growing from his nose. Easily the silliest entry but also the funniest.

The final story, *Eye*, was not directed by Carpenter but by fellow horror filmmaker Tobe Hooper. Hooper was, of course, the man behind the wonderful independent classic *The Texas Chain Saw Massacre* (1974). *Eye* is a reworking of *Mad Love* (1935) or *The Beast with Five Fingers* (1946) where the perils of transplanting a psychopath's body parts onto a normal patient have dire consequences. With stunning hallucinations and a well-orchestrated car crash, complete with messy consequences, this is an amiable episode.

Body Bags is a horror aficionado's dream, not just because of the script references but also the actors. The dead guy in the locker? That's Sam *'Evil Dead'* Raimi. One of the gas station customers is none other than Wes *'Scream'* Craven. Tobe Hooper is a morgue worker. The guru of low-budget horror, Roger Corman, plays the transplant specialist. There are also non-musical roles for Twiggy, Sheena Easton and Debbie

'*Videodrome*' Harry as well as Mark Hamill and David Warner. Overall, *Body Bags* may be a minor work but it never fails to entertain and, at its best, is more scary and tense than virtually any of its contemporaries.

Carpenter's next projects had their roots in classic science fiction and horror literature. In 1988 he had been approached by Michael DeLuca, who had written a script for an intellectual horror film based ostensibly on the works of HP Lovecraft. At the time, Carpenter was interested in the concept but felt that the script wasn't quite right. By 1993, however, DeLuca had reworked the script and this time Carpenter felt that there was plenty of material to explore.

In the Mouth of Madness (1994)

Directed by: John Carpenter
Produced by: Sandy King
Written by: Michael DeLuca
Director of Photography: Gary Kibbe
Music: John Carpenter and Jim Lang
Cast: Sam Neill (John Trent), Julie Carmen (Linda Styles), Charlton Heston (Jackson Harglow), Jurgen Prochnow (Sutter Cane), David Warner (Dr Renn)
91 mins

'*What if Cane's work isn't fiction?*'

Stephen King may well earn more money before breakfast than you do in a year, but even his earnings are peanuts compared with those of Sutter Cane. Cane's latest book *Hobb's End Horror* has been flying off the shelves so quickly that his publishers can't print enough of them. His next opus *In the Mouth of Madness* is all set to knock 'em dead, the only problem being that Cane has disappeared along with the remaining part of his manuscript. The publishers want him back, but are keen to keep the investigation low-key. This is where John Trent comes in. John's an insurance man who specialises in busting people who register false claims and he's very good at it. He is certainly clued in enough to realise that his part in the investigation could well be a publicity stunt to boost sales into the stratosphere, until he notices that the covers of Cane's novels piece together to make a map of New Hampshire. If it is a publicity stunt, it's going a bit far when Cane's agent tries to attack John with an axe in a coffee shop. Teaming up with editor Linda Styles, John heads off for Hobb's End as indicated on his map, a town not noted on any other. If the journey was strange, the town itself is something else. 'The place is picture perfect and there's nobody around.' Even the hotel is weird: the painting in reception keeps changing and the lady behind the counter looks just like the sort of person who would chop her naked husband into tiny pieces with an axe. Still, the view from the window is nice – rolling plains complete with the ominous, black-domed Orthodox church. The locals, too, are eager to welcome outsiders with sharpened blades and mysterious mob gatherings. With the prospect of discovering Cane becoming more likely and less desirable by the minute, John is rapidly discovering that perhaps the divide between fantasy and reality is disintegrating. All the future holds is madness, not just for John but for the millions of people who read Cane's books...

Films based on the works of HP Lovecraft crop up every once in a while but are normally pale shadows of the morbid writer's better stories. *The Dunwich Horror* (1970) and *The Unnameable* (1988) try but feel insipid, while Stuart Gordon's *Re-Animator* (1985) and *From Beyond* (1986) are enjoyable but lack the seriousness and madness of their sources. *In the Mouth of Madness*, while not adapted from specific Lovecraft stories, nevertheless carries the spirit of Lovecraft's work. Structurally, the inspiration comes from *The Case of Charles Dexter Ward* with its asylum book-ending and mental condition resulting from shock encounters with unspeakable entities. There are many more allusions, notably the evil in the black church setting of *The Hunter in the Dark* ('This place had once been the scene of an evil older than mankind and wider than the universe, it was a place of pain and suffering beyond human comprehension') and the title of Cane's new book relating to the Cthulhu novel *At the Mountains of Madness*. While not specifically mentioning any of the pantheon of Elder Ones that make up the Cthulhu mythos, the implications are clear. Lovecraft's skill as a horror writer (or conceit if you are a detractor) is that he rarely described the horrors – to see a god in the flesh would drive the observer and reader insane. For most of the film, Carpenter wisely sticks to the policy of not showing the full horror, preferring to rely on dripping and splashing blood, half-second flashes, the twitch of a tentacle or the strain upon a door. However, presumably because contemporary horror audiences don't always appreciate a subtle approach, there comes a time when he has to show the beast. Inevitably, it's a touch disappointing, not because the effects are poor but because what is revealed cannot match the nastiness of the anticipation. It's a common problem in horror cinema, although *The Thing* is an obvious exception. When the Elder Ones are unleashed and chase John down the corridor we are given, finally, the opportunity to see their horrors and they appear familiar – not the swish-tentacled monstrosities we may have expected but gnash-toothed, spindly-handed grotesques of the kind that populate Clive Barker's *Hellraiser* (1987) or *Night Breed* (1990). Cane's bestseller *Hobb's End Horror* mirrors the setting of the violent supernatural happenings perpetrated by an ancient alien race in Nigel Kneale's *Quatermass and the Pit*.

Carpenter has called *In the Mouth of Madness* the final part of his Apocalypse Trilogy, and there is certainly a thread that links the films. *The Thing* is an alien who crashed to earth before mankind was born and threatens the very existence of humankind should it escape its isolated location. By the film's close it seems as though disaster has been avoided – narrowly. *Prince of Darkness* extends this theme to an urban setting where contagious ancient evil is more virulent but apparently thwarted by the film's close. *In the Mouth of Madness*, however, takes the apocalypse to the edge and makes sure it goes right over. There is no doubt that this marks a serious breakdown in social order – thus each film becomes more nihilistic than the last.

The idea that reading a book or watching a film can lead to violent behaviour and psychosis is not a new one and is normally cited by the very people who want to stop the public watching horror films. Lovecraft's premise that seeing or being exposed to an ancient being can turn the mind to Jello is a common theme within his writing but also connects with William Burroughs' statement that 'Language is a virus from outer space'. The book is a plague carrier for an alien virus that is being unleashed upon the world. 'For years I thought I was making all this up, but they were telling me what to write,' confesses Cane. 'All those horrible and slimy things trying to get back in, they're all true.' In the uncompleted manuscript of Cane's book his editor is driven to madness because she can see what will happen to Trent and the rest of the world – she and Cane's agent are the only people who have read the book. This is the reason for having the flashback structure. She tries to warn Trent but is unable, because her destiny – her death and attempts to thwart Trent – are also part of the book. Later, the hope that perhaps people who don't read books may escape the danger is thwarted when it is revealed that the movie version is due to be released, the very film that we, the audience, are now watching. Carpenter is implicating himself in the contagion by suggesting that his films can cause imitative violence. This is the big joke – *In the Mouth of Madness* is exactly the kind of horror film that is unlikely to invoke what it purports. Carpenter criticises the argument that films force people to behave in certain ways by suggesting that his film could do so.

In many respects this is an unusual film for Carpenter stylistically, the editing is generally speedier than his normal languid pace and the narrative structured as one long flashback. Occasionally we get very swift cuts from the present (film time) to events that occur in the past or future, bombarding the characters and audiences with a barrage of images to reflect chaos and madness. The camera angles are also more skewed to reflect John's fractured psychosis and the colours more intense, searing the images onto the screen. Repetition is employed to disorientate and cloud our recollections. Early on in the film when John sees a policeman savagely beating a man in an alley we see the event again almost immediately but catch more than a glimpse of the policeman and view him as a hideous minion of the elder ones. This image is repeated several times in slightly different ways. The editing and shooting structure seems to be saying that we should question what we see and what we remember; memory is subjective in the sense that two people reading the same book will have different perceptions of what they have read. Connected with this is the scene where John tries to drive away from the confines of the town only to find himself repeatedly facing the same mob. We are told that this is because events have been written like that. His interpretation of what he sees may alter but the actuality cannot. For such a temporally complex film with nested structures and dreams within dreams, it is some surprise to find that it is not difficult to follow, which reflects Carpenter's skill as a storyteller.

The soundtrack, while sticking to genre stalwarts such as drips, creaks, groans and screams, is notably different to Carpenter's previous films. The score is less rhythmic and does not have the driving thematic leitmotifs that are so distinctive in his work. This has the effect, along with half-heard moans and snatches of electronica, of disorientating the viewer further as there is far less familiar material to latch on to. At times the soundtrack, like the picture and the editing, warps and distorts to further give the audience the impression of fractured reality. The use of pre-recorded songs adds humour to the film – for example, the opening features The Carpenters' *We've Only Just Begun*, which might be viewed as literally true (the film has only just begun) but, considering the temporal distortion on show, acts as an ironic commentary on the film we are about to see.

In the Mouth of Madness proved to be an interesting project, an attempt at a different kind of horror with an intelligent edge, like *Prince of Darkness*. Unfortunately, lacklustre distribution meant that it wasn't successful enough to start any trends and it remains an interesting curio.

Continuing with the literary theme, Carpenter was given the opportunity to remake John Wyndham's classic *The Midwich Cuckoos* as *Village of the Damned*.

Village of the Damned (1995)

Directed by: John Carpenter
Produced by: Sandy King and Michael Preger
Written by: David Himmelstein based on The Midwich Cuckoos by John Wyndham
Director of Photography: Gary Kibbe
Music: John Carpenter and Dave Davies
Cast: Christopher Reeve (Alan Chaffee), Kirstie Alley (Dr Susan Verner), Mark Hamill (Rev George), Michael Paré (Frank), Linda Kozlowski (Jill McGowan), Lindsey Haun (Mara)
99 mins

Alan's antenatal clinic has become a lot more popular recently. This is mainly because his sleepy little village has undergone a group conception that has affected a large proportion of the female population. It all happened one morning whilst Alan was out of town. At 10 o'clock on the dot the whole of Midwich went into a deep trance. As suddenly as it had started it was over, leaving a sizeable number of pregnant women and intense government interest in local politics. It's deeply suspicious as the children all have the same genetic make-up – 'almost as if they are siblings from the same parent.' Born with distinctive features, silver hair and bright eyes, they are also highly intelligent, act as a group and are more than a little creepy. If that wasn't enough to arouse suspicion, the spate of accidents that follow the little darlings wherever they go certainly raises the odd eyebrow. Barbara, Alan's wife, plummets to her death following a nasty incident involving telepathic autosuggestion and a pan of boiling water. Others follow and, before long, the entire village is at the mercy of the children, who can read minds and act as a collective consciousness. Their ascendancy seems inevitable, brutal and unstoppable.

Village of the Damned had been made before by Wolf Rilla in 1960 and also as *Children of the Damned* (1963), a black-and-white British film directed by Anton M Leader. Based upon John Wyndham's controversial (at the time) novel *The Midwich Cuckoos* (1957), Carpenter's version updates the theme to a modern, isolated American village. The underlying horror comes from the women of the village being unknowingly violated and follows the breakdown of a community because of the effects of mass rape. No direct explanation is given; we don't know where the children came from but we are sure that their purpose is malevolent. Despite being alien, their ultimate defence is that, like in *Invasion of the Body Snatchers* (1955), they look like us. More than that, they appear to be 'children', which creates a number of screen taboos – children having the propensity to carry out malicious acts and also that of premeditated violence against children. We all know that children are not 'little angels' but filmmakers normally shy away from such depictions for fear of offending sensibilities. Carpenter plays on the audience's predisposition to stereotype children in a number of his films: the 'vanilla twist' girl in *Assault on Precinct 13*; the cannibalistic and dog-munching kids (more taboos than you can shake a stick at) in *In the Mouth of Madness*. It's made slightly more palatable by leaving the audience in no doubt that they are evil; as we watch them force their parents to commit suicide, we experience no feelings of ambiguity. Linked with this is their spooky appearance, which instantly puts them beyond everyday expectation. 'Eyes are the windows of the soul' and this is shown to be apt for the Midwich children – their stares are cold and empty. Their expression doesn't alter when they commit each atrocity; they are incapable of feeling – 'Emotion is irrelevant, it is not our nature.' Their cruelties are petty, unnecessary and childish. By focusing on the eyes, the viewer is given the opportunity to stare into the abyss as it stares back. When the children unleash their powers we are shown an extreme close-up of the eyes as they change colour, dilate and mutate.

Distrust of authority manifests itself in *Village of the Damned* almost from the opening. As soon as the village comes under the 10 o'clock freeze we witness the laughable actions of the local police, sending a man into the area only to have him drop down and sleep as soundly as the cows in the adjacent field. However, it takes a big government organisation to be truly abusive of personal freedoms. The aliens declare that 'it isn't a matter of hate; it is a matter of biological observation'. The government are shown to have the same attitude, especially through the actions of the truly sinister Dr Verner. The alien biogenesis may be down to scientific observation of an inferior species by an emotionless race, but governmental experimentation is a betrayal of trust of their own species. The government are two-faced, offering $3,000 a month for the women to keep babies that they may not want purely so that they can observe the phenomenon. That they didn't need to offer the sweetener – all the women insisted on keeping the babies due to psychically transmitted requests from their embryos – is irrelevant. The authorities realise early on that the children are a threat and it is clear that this situation has occurred before, which is why they are so prepared and swift in their response. But in the end even they admit defeat, sending in the armed forces – who prove to be just as ineffectual. In *Village of the Damned* it is intelligence that wins out. Alan manages to use his mind rather than brute force to defeat the children. He realises that having the body of a human doesn't equate to having human spirit. In this way the children are as 'lifeless' as the killer child robots in Philip K Dick's *Screamers* (also made into a film in 1995).

John Carpenter makes a cameo appearance early on in the film as a man standing in a telephone booth, noted in the credits under the pseudonym Rip Haight. Distribution for the film was disappointingly small and managed to bypass cinemas in the UK. Fortunately the DVD release means that you can enjoy *Village of the Damned* in the privacy of your own home. With the kids...

Ever since the success of the original film there had been plans to make a sequel to *Escape from New York*. Kurt Russell, Debra Hill and Carpenter were all keen to see Snake Plissken's return to the big screen. After two relatively low-key projects Carpenter managed to secure a budget of $50 million from Paramount. Because of the length of time that had elapsed since the original film, it was decided that *Escape from LA* would be a standalone film, so as not to alienate a youth audience who may have been unfamiliar with the original.

Escape from LA (1996)

Directed by: John Carpenter
Produced by: Debra Hill and Kurt Russell
Written by: John Carpenter, Debra Hill and Kurt Russell
Director of Photography: Gary Kibbe
Music: John Carpenter and Shirley Walker
Cast: Kurt Russell (Snake Plissken), Steve Buscemi ('Map to the Stars' Eddie), Peter Fonda (Pipeline), Pam Grier (Hershe), Stacy

Keach (Malloy), Bruce Campbell (Surgeon General of Beverley Hills), AJ Langer (Utopia), George Corraface (Cuervo Jones), Michelle Forbes (Braxen)
100 mins

2013. Now. Los Angeles has been cut off from the rest of the US coastline in the 'quake of 2000' following a period of massive civil unrest. The lifetime president of the United States has instigated a radical policy of sending undesirables, immigrants, those lacking wholesome moral fibre or, heaven forbid, atheists to be extradited to LA Island. Once you go in, you don't come out. Bad news, then, for Mr President when his errant daughter Utopia goes AWOL, stealing an important black box and using an escape pod to land in LA, straight into the arms of her paramour Cuervo Jones, a self-styled rebel rouser with a Che Guevara fixation. Jones is leader of the Shining Path, an affiliation of nations determined to bring down America. The future of the world is at stake because the black box contains a dinky CD that enables the user to control a belt of satellites which can switch off the power in any country, or take out the entire world. Who can be given the monumental task of saving mankind? Following a failed attempt to rescue the CD (but not the daughter) by a crack team of commandos, it's clear that there's only one man for the job – twice decorated, one-eyed, tattooed wisecracker Snake Plissken, which is convenient as he's about to be shipped to LA on account of an astonishing 27 immoral actions. The incentive? A clean slate for his misdemeanours and an antidote to Plutoxin 7, which is currently addling his body's defences, a virus deliberately administered to make him co-operate. Taking a turbo-charged nuclear submarine and armed to the teeth with a plethora of whizzy gadgets, he sets about recovering the black box. But with the whole of LA's bizarre gangs and sinister cults against him plus a paltry ten-hour deadline between him and his goal, the prospects do not look good.

'The United States is a no-smoking nation. No smoking. No drinking. No drugs. No women, unless – of course – you are married. No guns. No foul language. No red meat.'

Plissken returns! From the opening mix of *Escape from New York*'s theme tune we are most certainly back with the Snake. Fifteen years on, both in film time and actual time, we are told about the intervening years courtesy of a condensed history from a female voiceover. Sounds familiar? Well, it is, because *Escape from LA* isn't so much a sequel as a re-run of its predecessor – bigger, louder, dumber, its patent formula of road-movie set-pieces and a tight time limit echoing the rule 'if it ain't broke, don't fix it'. While this approach means that *Escape from LA* is an enjoyable science-fiction action romp, it does beg inevitable comparisons with the original and sadly finds itself wanting. While it ups the ante in terms of ludicrous set-pieces and playful gadgets, giving it the feel of a more upbeat, less grimy punk film, the overall message is unremittingly grim, topping the nihilistic aspects of the first. The intervening period has seen the forced rise of the far right in American politics. Clearly this extremism fits uneasily with the liberal individualism of Plissken. His right to smoke becomes as important an issue of individual liberty as his right to freedom. Taslima explains to Snake why the harsh life in LA is preferable to the America the disenfranchised have left behind – they may be trapped but ultimately have more freedom inside a prison than out of it. Cuervo is as brutal as the ostensibly squeaky-clean President he hopes to depose and just as much a dictator. His control over Utopia (in VR dreams as in *Prince of Darkness* and *Village of the Damned*) mirrors the Patty Hearst incident but also makes clear his motives. Given the choice between these two forms of slavery, both left and right wing, Snake takes the most extreme option. Instead of choosing between his country that has rejected him and other countries that do not care for him, he takes them all out. The world is plunged into darkness because Snake has an attitude and believes in personal liberty. If he can't have freedom then nobody can.

Of course, if *Escape from LA* was a non-stop depressing treatise on politics it wouldn't work as an action film. Instead, the narrative compensates for the depressing outlook by depicting an increasingly bizarre and preposterous array of spectacles that segue breathlessly from one to another. And even when matters are grim they are played with such a high degree of gallows humour that you laugh rather than wince. It is a combination of careful angles, effects work and well-timed editing that set the action sequences apart. Plissken first gets the opportunity to meet with Cuervo during the parade. Does he walk up and introduce himself? Of course not. Instead, he jumps a motorbike and careers off in pursuit, guns down some henchmen, wrenches one off a bike, crashes all manner of vehicles and flies onto the back of a moving truck. Climbing along the roof he clings on for dear life and takes out a cowboy in an increasingly desperate bid to reach his target. The result of these heroics? Taken down by Cuervo's well-aimed bolas and dragged off to be shot by four armed henchmen, he manages to avoid this fate by judicious use of a tin can and some cheating. Bangkok rules indeed. Then he and the ill-fated Taslima are captured by a black-cassocked monk firing nets and dragged off to meet the Surgeon General of Beverley Hills (played with plastic-faced insanity by cult *Evil Dead* actor Bruce Campbell) who wants to use their healthy body parts to patch up the desperate hordes of plastic-surgery victims.

Bruce Campbell is not the only familiar face among the crowd. Steve Buscemi plays 'Map to the Stars' Eddie, a dodgy wheeler dealer with a cheesy recorded guidebook to areas of Hollywood. Pam Grier of *Foxy Brown* (1974), *Coffy* (1973) and *Jackie Brown* (1997) fame plays Hershe, aka Carjack Malone, an ex-partner of Snake's who has changed sex but retained the gruff voice. Paul

Bartel, director of the wonderful *Eating Raoul* (1982), appears as a commissioner, but the finest extended cameo is that of Peter Fonda as a Californian hippy slacker surfer.

If you hadn't seen the original this would be one helluva hoot, but the feeling of *déjà vu* is at times overwhelming. The prison concept is the same, the mission is to recover a CD rather than a tape (how technology changes), Snake is duped into the mission and receives a potentially fatal injection, he has a tracer that occasionally doesn't work, the first thing he finds is a macabre red herring and the mode of transport for getting in and out of the city is destroyed, cutting off the planned escape route. Someone close to the baddie occasionally double crosses him but turns out to be alright and the captor is a gang leader with an unusually modified car. After capture, Snake faces 'certain death' in a gladiatorial arena spurred on by a hostile crowd. Snake meets a girl who recognises him, offers to go to bed with him and is promptly killed. And, of course, everyone he meets recognises him and repeats a stock phrase, 'I heard you were dead' now being replaced with 'I thought you'd be taller'. What *Escape from New York* didn't have, though, was a hysterically camp, pantomime-violence showdown featuring Snake, Hershe and the gang strapped to leather hang-gliders while butchering the Shining Path's gang members in their droves – and distracting them with that old chestnut 'he's behind you'.

Despite the best efforts of the colourful panavision cinematography, *Escape from LA* is actually less convincing effects-wise than its cheaper sibling. Partly this is due to the scale and extent of the filmmaking – *Escape from LA* has so many sets and effects sequences that the sheer quantity makes the undertaking far more intense. The first 20 minutes alone feature a bewildering variety of images – the impressive destruction of LA, large-scale riots, matte and model shots, wire-frame displays, holographic projections that Snake runs right through, a nuclear submarine and its subsequent lengthy underwater journey through the derelict parts of flooded LA (complete with Universal Studios' *Jaws* pastiche), video effects of Cuervo in a virtual diary as well as military hardware, crashes and more composite shots than are strictly necessary. But the main problem is that the effects used in some of these sequences are necessarily CGI. The problem with CGI as opposed to conventional effects work is that, being in its infancy at the time, it had a tendency to date quickly.

Escape from LA was the second part of a planned trilogy for Plissken, but from where could he escape next time? A rumoured final instalment was to see Plissken *Escape from Earth*. Despite the muted reception accorded *Escape from LA*, interest in Plissken as a cult character has not waned – there are Plissken dolls, rumours of a prequel or a remake of the original *Escape from New York* at the time of writing, and an homage to the perennially scowling anti-hero can be seen in the continuing adventures of computer game character Solid Snake. Whether *Escape from Earth* ever materialises remains to be seen.

In 1997 Carpenter was offered the chance to adapt John Steakley's novel *Vampire$*. It gave him the opportunity to film in the western setting of Santa Fe. The vampire film is a staple part of the horror genre but one that offers a great degree of malleability even as its subject matter is familiar. As such, many directors have had a stab at making vampire films because they offer the opportunity to play with genre conventions. Typically, Carpenter approached the material from a fresh and unexpected perspective.

John Carpenter's Vampires (1998)

Directed by: John Carpenter
Produced by: Sandy King
Written by: Dan Jakoby from the book *Vampire$* by John Steakley

Director of Photography: Gary Kibbe
Music: John Carpenter
Cast: James Woods (Jack Crow), Thomas Ian Griffith (Valek), Daniel Baldwin (Montoya), Sheryl Lee (Katrina), Tim Guinee (Father Adam), Maximilian Schell (Cardinal Alba)
103mins

Introducing Jack Crow – killer, bad attitude, mid-40s. Also introducing Jan Valek – killer, bad attitude, mid-600s. Now Jack don't get on with most people, but with Valek it's a whole new thing of not getting along. You see, Valek is a vampire and Jack's business is killing them on behalf of the Holy Roman Church, a profession he takes very seriously. Travelling the length and breadth of the country with his crack team of hunters and incumbent priest, he searches for vampire nests and orchestrates their destruction with venomous zeal. The latest find in a disused shack in the middle of nowhere is a bit of a mystery as there is no master vampire – 'Rule #5: If you find the nest, you find the master.' All becomes clear later that night when missing master Valek gatecrashes the after-barbecue knees up and mercilessly slaughters all in his wake: hunters, the padre and even the prostitutes. More by luck than judgement, the only people left alive are Jack, Montoya and a prostitute named Katrina. Katrina has sustained a bite from Valek and runs a very good chance of becoming subservient to his will, something that Jack and Montoya can use to their advantage as she is now effectively a human compass pointing in the direction of the master vamp. Jack is pretty sure that he's been set up – Valek knew his name – and, eager to cut through the bullshit he's been fed by the Vatican, Jack demands to know the rap on the vamp. A former priest who turned against the church and was later burned for heresy in the 1300s, it turns out that Valek is the first recorded vampire, the master of all masters. Now he's in America on a mission to find the Black Cross, an artefact whose power, it is said, will invest in vampires the ability to walk unharmed in the sunlight. If vampires are difficult to kill now, then the removal of one of their only weaknesses would tip the balance entirely in their favour. All that stands in Valek's way is a long road, a ramshackle monastery and Jack Crow.

Strange though it may seem, while Carpenter has made films based upon westerns and has a clear enthusiasm for the genre, he has never directed one himself. *Vampires* is the closest he comes, but once again genre cross-fertilisation is apparent. He admits that this is 'essentially *The Wild Bunch* meets Vlad the Impaler'. It takes the elements of the western that involve the resolution of order within a portrayed society or group, but subverts them by combining this with a road movie and, of course, vampires. The premise is minimal – in a basic quest scenario we have good guys facing bad guys and no need for a subplot, deep introspection or psychological analysis. Vampires exist; they need to be destroyed.

Once again, in Crow we find the Hawksian male, part of the system working for the Catholic church, but he is very much his own man. In this case, it's a solid dose of revenge that he seeks – he became a hunter because both his parents were vampire victims. He even had to kill his own father. However, when his team are wiped out and the church begins behaving decidedly suspiciously towards him, he has to start anew. Crow breaks the rules. The slayers have a rigid code of conduct to ensure their safety, but each time Montoya reminds him of the rules, another one falls by the wayside. Crow disobeys the cardinal's orders to reform the team and sets off, with Montoya and a naïve padre, to destroy Valek using Katrina as a psychic guide. The relationship between Crow and Montoya is fundamental – both loyal to each other, the first and most important rule for the slayers is that, if any one of them is bitten, his comrades are to destroy him. When Montoya turns, Jack's hatred of vampirism is temporarily quashed through a deep respect for his colleague. *Vampires* has been accused of misogyny, particularly in its treatment of Katrina, and it's hard to disagree. In many respects the film is about tough men doing a tough job. None of the slayers are pleasant or compassionate and, to Jack, the ends always justify the means no matter how unacceptable they appear to be.

Carpenter has dabbled with supernatural elements in many of his films – from the Shape in *Halloween* through to the Devil in *Prince of Darkness* and Sutter Cane's bizarre creatures from *In the Mouth of Madness*; the fascination lies with the ordinary hero confronting and defeating extraordinary powers. Vampire mythology is re-imagined on a film-by-film basis and, as the title makes abundantly clear, these really are John Carpenter's vampires. Crow emphasises this when he sets the record straight with the new padre – 'Forget what you've seen in the movies' – and quickly goes on to dispel many traditional vampire myths: crosses and garlic are no good here. Despite sporting a fine set of fangs, Valek doesn't seem to do very much conventional biting either; apart from seducing Katrina by nibbling between her legs, the rest of the time he's more a supernatural killing machine, ripping bodies in two with his bare hands or decapitating victims with a single blow. He is, however, vulnerable in the daylight and wise enough to know that diurnal self-burial is a pretty good method of avoiding both sunlight and slayers. One of the common themes of vampirism is that of disease – victims become contaminated by it. Extreme measures are required not only to destroy the vampire, but to cleanse the putrefaction. Any contact with vampires must result in burning and decapitation. Indeed, as the team of slayers purge the nest, stakes are no good other than to drag the undead, kicking and screaming, into the bright sunshine, whereupon they spontaneously combust in a crowd-pleasing luminescent flame. After the team of hunters are killed by Valek, Crow performs the same ritual. When Montoya is bitten by Katrina, however, the ritual moves into parody as he initially burns his arm with a lighter then later fires a machine-gun into the air, allowing the heat from the barrel to cauterise the wound. Another recurring vampire theme lies in the realm of immortality. Valek himself is over 600 years old and can offer the prospect of eternal life – a temptation that is too great for an ageing priest. 'You are truly a pile of dogshit, Cardinal,' notes Jack.

The soundtrack is mainly guitar-based with a strong bass theme which is appropriate for the setting. Carpenter had five weeks to score the film (compared to three days for *Halloween*!), which he did with an impressive array of famous blues musicians, but not all of the compositions are his – one is a piece of music written and performed by his then 13-year-old son Cody. The music when they approach the town at the climax is based on the stifling Mexican music in *Rio Bravo*. Visually Carpenter has once again pulled out all the stops; the cinematography, in particular, is gorgeous, with deep-red filters emphasising the arrival of the ominous sunsets, although in fact all the dusk scenes were shot during daylight. The scene where the vampires emerge from the ground was co-ordinated by radio as the actors really were buried, with special breathing boxes – the scene had to be shot several times in the blazing sun as sometimes they couldn't all stand up properly. Surprisingly, there was no extensive use of CGI and most of the effects were performed in-camera, the only digital trickery involving wire-removal work in the climactic fight between Crow and Valek.

A sequel, *Vampires: Los Muertos* (2002), executive produced by Carpenter, is clearly a lower-budget answer to the original with Carpenter regular Tommy Lee Wallace writing and directing, whilst Jon Bon Jovi takes the reins as the lead vampire hunter, the unfortunately named Derek Bliss. Receiving assignments from the Internet and recording kills on his camera, Bliss has set himself up as a sucker-exterminating franchise. A lucrative deal sees him join a rapidly diminishing team of vampire hunters in search of a powerful female vampire leader. The plentiful gore (owing much to Romero's *Living Dead* films) and a kooky cast of sidekicks (the mysterious Goth girl, the kid, the suspicious monks) make sure things never flag. While many of the scenes are repeated wholesale from the original, there are still plenty of twists to keep things fresh, with strange rituals and potential cures for the affliction set against the glaring – vampire unfriendly – Mexican sun and the dingy comic-book lighting of underground crypts and garish streets. Carpenter had no involvement with the third film, *Vampires: The Turning* (2005), which moved the action to Thailand.

Ghosts of Mars (2001)

Directed by: John Carpenter
Produced by: John Carpenter and Sandy King
Written by: John Carpenter and Larry Sulkis
Director of Photography: Gary Kibbe
Music: John Carpenter
Cast: Natasha Henstridge (Melanie Ballard), Ice Cube (James 'Desolation' Williams), Pam Grier (Helena), Danielle Burgio (Local Cop), Joanna Cassidy (Whitlock), Clea DuVall (Bashira Kincaid), Harry Jay Knowles (A Head on a Pike)
98 mins

'I didn't say I was innocent. I just didn't kill nobody.'

2176. Mars. Something that has been buried for centuries has just been uncovered.

Lt Melanie Ballard is found, bound, onboard an otherwise empty train that has bolted out of the Martian mining city of Chryse. There are traces of tetromonochloride in her system, a cause for concern. Naturally, an explanation is required and the lieutenant, injured but conscious, is able to narrate the horrific series of events that have led to her current situation in front of a jury. It all began with a routine prison transfer of notorious criminal James 'Desolation' Williams…

Melanie and a small team catch the train to Chryse but, when they arrive, things are clearly very wrong. At first the town seems a desolate wasteland but, on entering the prison, they are greeted by the grizzly sight of blood-spattered walls, severed limbs and rows of decapitated bodies hanging from the ceilings. Initially it seems likely that the deaths could fit Desolation Williams' modus operandi, but when they find him securely locked in his cell they realise that they face a challenge that is far from human. Despite their obvious concerns, they are forced to team up with both the prisoners and any survivors who are still sane. But what is the threat that they face? Whitlock, an archaeologist who worked around the mine area, seems to have an explanation: an excavation revealed ancient ruins beneath the Martian surface but also unleashed a crimson gas, comprising the spirits of aeons-old Martians, which possessed the workers. Those that succumbed formed a deadly gang. Those that did not change were brutally murdered. Humans have no place on Mars; the ghosts that have lain dormant in the depths of the planet are now awakened and eager to repel the infection of their world. Nothing, it seems, can stop them, for if you kill one, you only destroy the host – the spirit is free to possess another victim. The odds for the increasingly depleted group diminish and their only hope is to get back to the train and get the hell out of there. But that doesn't solve the problem of the ghosts of Mars, and perhaps running away isn't necessarily the most honourable solution, with a spiritual and physical apocalypse threatening the planet.

If you were to take all the elements of John Carpenter's oeuvre and try to fit as many of them as possible into one film then you'd probably end up with something like *Ghosts of Mars*. Firstly, it's a science-fiction film set in the future. There's the *Assault on Precinct 13* plot about a notorious prisoner joining with his captors to fight a greater threat. There's the sense of paranoia about identity from *The Thing*, possession from *Prince of Darkness*, ghost stories from *The Fog*, sudden scares from *Halloween*, and the post-apocalyptic punk sensibility of *Escape from New York*. It's all there and more besides, with typically growling dialogue to boot. So, in effect, *Ghosts of Mars* is the ultimate genre movie – a supernatural science-fiction horror western filled with gore, stunts and action from start to finish. It's not art; it's not meant to be. Unfortunately, though, *Ghosts of Mars* never quite lives up to the sum of its parts and partly, rather like *Vampires*, the blame can be laid on the structure. Playing around with narrative time can be an effective tool (see much of Quentin Tarantino's work or Carpenter's *In the Mouth of Madness*) but the flashback-within-flashback structure here feels unnecessary and muddled. Meanwhile, the evocative cinematography, all moody reds and browns, is compromised by the stylistic use of cross-fading editing (also a feature in *Vampires*, although used to a lesser extent), which becomes quite irritating. That said, when the film does succeed, it really goes for the jugular, often quite literally.

In many ways, *Ghosts of Mars* is a strange film in that it tries very hard to match the sensibilities of a 1970s/80s action genre film with the expectations of 2001's cinema mores. Traditionally, horror films tend to be moody and/or gory while action films have relied on stunts and body count. *Ghosts of Mars* tries to blend the two together in a science-fiction environment, rather like Paul Verhoeven did with *Starship Troopers* (1997). The results are varied with some scenes recalling the 'Crazies' sequence from *Escape from New York* intercut with astonishing and brutal decapitations courtesy of the ever reliable KNB EFX Group. This really shows the film's cutting-edge use of prosthetic effects as a bewildering number of body parts fly across the screen. The tribal group themselves are a welcome return to the post-apocalyptic, body-pierced grunge anarchists as popularised by *Escape from New York* and also *Mad Max 2*, rhythmically banging metallic shields to psyche themselves up for another attack on the unpossessed. Accompanying all this mayhem is a new twist on the John Carpenter soundtrack. As we have already seen, the soundtrack is one of the defining elements of a Carpenter film. *Ghosts of Mars* is, however, a bit different. Although he composed the main score, the final recorded soundtrack comprised collaborations between a series of guest musicians performing over his already laid down compositions. Anthrax, the legendary Steve Vai and eccentric composer/guitarist Buckethead all contributed to the project, producing one of the most shred-heavy original soundtracks yet heard. It's an interesting way of mixing the controlled minimalism of Carpenter's work with the kind of thrash music that typically underscores the modern grunge action-horror film. It is also a departure from films which employ their metal-inspired accompaniments as off-the-shelf pieces designed to shift tie-in CDs.

The bulk of filming was shot at night in New Mexico at a gypsum mine owned by the Sovereign Indian Nation of the Pueblo of Zia with the distinctive red earth of the Martian landscape created by spray-painting the white gypsum with dye. Although many of the shots are composited using a combination of modelwork and CGI a large part of the action was completed in-camera, old school style, by a bewildering number of stunt people hurled across the sets by hidden air rams or crashing specially modified vehicles through exploding debris. Although these are still dangerous to perform, and modern action films seem to require an increasing number of stunts to satiate their audience, technology does offer some distinct safety advantages; many of the handheld weapons thrown at and into the actors were digitally rendered in post-production. The most elaborate use of effects occurs in the sequences set on and around the train. The complication comes from the marrying of three distinct effects styles in a way that is transparent – the train itself was a combination of a (partly built) full scale set, a rendered CGI version and a model version with different combinations used for various shots. The actors were later green-screened into these environments.

Despite its reasonable budget ($30 million fell into that strange gulf between big-budget Hollywood and low-budget independent filmmaking) and interest in its cast, *Ghosts of Mars* failed to make a notable impact on the world box office, instead proving more lucrative as a superior action DVD rental. It's a shame as, whatever its faults, it is, like most of Carpenter's work, best appreciated on a big screen. *Ghosts of Mars* takes pretty much every theme and direction from Carpenter's previous films and mixes them all up in a cross-genre cavalcade of smart-arsed dialogue and violence. Unfortunately, the end results are muddled and old fashioned, but still enjoyable.

After a hiatus of four years, Carpenter returned to the director's chair with two episodes for the Masters of Horror series. Starting as an idea at a casual dining club for like-minded directors of horror, TV director Mick Garris (*The Stand*, *The Shining*) came up with an elegant solution to the endless moans about MPAA interference and lack of studio interest in the genre – make what you want and release it on video. Thus Masters of Horror was born: single films of an hour in length, restricted only by budget and shooting schedule. Budget issues were eased slightly when Showtime came on board to broadcast the films although they did add some restrictions regarding male nudity and child-on-child violence. Carpenter was in good company – other directors involved with the project were some of his contemporaries including Tobe Hooper, Dario Argento, John Landis and Joe Dante, plus some younger directors, such as Miike Takashi. Thirteen episodes were commissioned for each season and the guaranteed 'no studio interference' clause was honoured, though Showtime did not air the Miike Takashi episode.

John Carpenter's Cigarette Burns (2005)

Directed by: John Carpenter
Written by: Drew McWeeny, Scott Swan
Music by: Cody Carpenter
Cast: Norman Reedus (Kirby), Udo Kier (Bellinger), Gary Hetherington (Walter), Zara Taylor (Annie)
59 mins

Kirby Sweetman is in trouble. His cinema isn't pulling in the punters and, what's more, it isn't even his, bought on loan from his dead junkie wife's dad, Walter, who now wants his $200,000 back. Kirby's sideline in financing his venture is tracing rare films for discerning collectors and his latest client, Bellinger, is most discerning. He is also willing to pay $200,000 to trace the celluloid of his desire. And the film he wants is the only print of *La fin absolue du monde* by obsessive director Hans Backovic. But this film has a powerful hold over those who seek it and an even greater one over those who have seen it – the only official showing resulted in carnage. But Bellinger doesn't care; he knows he's going to hell so wants one glimpse of heaven, as mirrored in the pitiful angel, whose wings have been cruelly hacked off, that he keeps shackled in his mansion.

Cigarette Burns recalls the Lovecraftian stylings of *In the Mouth of Madness* and *Prince of Darkness* in the way that it plays with characters' reality and perception of supernatural forces. Central to the film is the Necronomicon substitute *La fin absolue du monde*, a celluloid MacGuffin whose constant reference is the film's only weak point – the repetition detracts from the narrative flow. The cigarette burns of the title are a neat allusion that works on a number of levels – they are reel markers on films, indicate the onset of horrific visions and refer to the endless fags puffed at by many Carpenter protagonists. In many ways this is a defiant film in the face of increasing conservatism in the film industry and increasing Puritanism from the establishment. *La fin absolue du monde* comes from the early 80s, just before Reaganism and Thatcherism decimated freedom of expression in pursuit of a moral crusade. These are lamented as better times, as reflected in Kirby's futile attempts at keeping a cinema business alive by showing great genre films (for example, Dario Argento's classic giallo *Deep Red*) as opposed to anodyne blockbusters. Also, the characters in this film smoke cigarettes, something that was flagged up as a worry in *Escape from LA* and is becoming increasingly censored.

Like *In the Mouth of Madness*, *Cigarette Burns* is knowingly self-referential about the process of filming and editing without being hip in its postmodernity. Film is shown as creating a bond between maker and audience, a relationship forged on mutual trust. We are told that Backovic 'abused that trust that we place in filmmakers', a line that absolves genre filmmakers from media witch hunts by placing the blame at the feet of a fictional bogeyman. The media's assertion that 'film violence equals real violence' is paradoxically proved to be correct, albeit for just one film. It is implied that Hollywood is the real enemy here, but there is an unholy alliance between those who applaud independent, free-thinking cinema and those who 'abuse the trust'. This is reinforced in the key scene when Kirby finds himself at the mercy of a snuff-movie maker, bound to watch a taxi driver being graphically decapitated by his captor. Clearly mirroring terrorist execution videos, the killer boasts proudly, 'One take. One uninterrupted shot. The only cut was to her. This is truth.' But the way the scene is shot (not from the point of view of the static camera) indicates that his pontifications are woefully off the mark – like *La fin absolue du monde* itself, the truth lies not in actuality but in artifice. Filmmaking is about telling lies 24 times a second. Carpenter reinforces this artificiality in the way he plays with jump cuts and deliberately jarring editing, both to shock the audience and also to draw attention to the construction of the film. *Cigarette Burns* offers a thoughtful examination of the role of the media and the manipulation of the viewer without getting bogged down with academic baggage. To compensate for the arguments about the nature of free speech and how the media manipulates audiences, there's also plentiful gore and shock moments as well as a fine performance from genre favourite Udo Kier. The soundtrack helps matters along with its simple interweaving piano lines recalling *Halloween* – the music was composed by Cody Carpenter.

Mixing elements of *The Ninth Gate* (1999) and the dreadful *8mm* (1999), *Cigarette Burns* is a satisfying hour of intelligent gore. Masters of Horror went on to a second, and final, season which Carpenter also contributed to.

Pro-Life (2006)

Directed by: John Carpenter
Written by: Drew McWeeny, Scott Swan
Music by: Cody Carpenter
Cast: Ron Perlman (Dwayne Burcell), Emmanuelle Vaugier (Kim), Mark Feuerstein (Alex), Caitlin Wachs (Angelique), Bill Dow (Dr Kiefer)
57 mins

'God wants you to kill my baby.'

On the way to work, Kim and Alex almost run over Angelique, a scared and nervous woman stumbling through the remote forests. Fearing for her health they take her to the Lincoln County Women's Health Service – coincidentally where they work as doctors. Not only is Angelique confused, she's also pregnant, a problem compounded by the fact that her father, Dwayne, is under a court injunction preventing him from entering the clinic's grounds. Not that the law seems to matter to Dwayne; he wants his daughter back come hell or high water. Angelique, meanwhile, is determined to have an abortion of the baby she claims was conceived the previous weekend – this despite clear indications that she is more heavily pregnant than her protestations indicate. As if things weren't bad enough, Angelique is only 15, meaning that her irate and fervently religious father has a say in her treatment. Alex, convinced that Dwayne raped his daughter, carries on regardless with his prognosis of what is beginning to be an increasingly bizarre pregnancy, the unborn child kicking like a pro-footballer and causing Angelique agony with its rapid growth. Dwayne and his three sons are determined to break into the clinic and get his daughter out – 'God requires us to take action.' He kills the guard and lays the hospital to siege, something a fully armed and flak-jacketed Dr Kiefer, the head of the clinic, is determined to curtail. The other doctors, meanwhile, try to keep the rapidly accelerating gestation of Angelique's baby under control – a baby Angelique believes is the result of demonic rape. She is willing to harm herself rather than be subjected to its rapidly approaching birth. And as if all that weren't enough, what will happen if the happy father comes to see his new-born son?

Carpenter's second contribution to Masters of Horror was once again written by Drew McWeeny and Scott Swan and initially entitled *Like Father, Like Son*. Like *Cigarette Burns*, this was to be a genre piece that tackled wider social issues. In *Cigarette Burns* the issue was about censorship and the effect of films on their viewers, but with *Pro-Life* the weighty issue of abortion was central to the story. Abortion has been a divisive issue in US politics ever since the case of Roe vs Wade in 1973 effectively gave women the right to choose, although the application of that decision varies substantially from state to state. It's a tremendously difficult argument to weigh up objectively in an hour, even given horror's reputation for delivering social commentary through metaphor. McWeeny and Swan soothe the irreconcilable divide by adding demonic elements to the screenplay – forcing the story into the realms of the fantastical.

Pro-Life tries to take in the difficult decisions made by teenage girls and their parents when faced with an unexpected pregnancy – showing that, in many ways, neither side is right or wrong. The determinedly steely Dwayne seems, on the surface, to be that genre staple, the bible-bashing, hellfire-and-brimstone hillbilly, quick to denounce those who have 'the entire history of children's genocide laid out under glass' with savage and fatal violence. To some extent he is that cartoonish figure, one whose eye-for-an-eye justice (he enacts his own bloody interpretation of abortion on the whimpering Dr Kiefer) is supplemented by his assertions that his actions are directly assigned from God. But he shows genuine love for his daughter by pleading, 'Please don't punish her, God. Please don't take my little girl,' when seeing her in the operating theatre after she has made it patently clear that she wants to abort the foetus. The doctor's actions are not entirely noble either – Alex refuses to listen to his patient's assertions about her condition. He is in many ways as pig-headed and blinkered as his nemesis.

Although the intentions of *Pro-Life* are aimed suitably high, the end result is a touch muddled – a case of over-egging the pudding with 'Carpenter stuff' as well as other horror tropes thrown in for good measure. There's the demonic birth (*Rosemary's Baby* mixed with the accelerated gestation of *Demon Seed*) of a child that looks like the head-crab from *The Thing* mixed with the killer baby of *It's Alive*. There's the *Assault on Precinct 13* siege and the *Prince of Darkness* devil (looking like the cover of a heavy metal album). Although it's an enjoyable and fast-paced production you can't help agreeing with Dwayne when he asserts, 'This doesn't make any sense.'

The soundtrack is once again provided by Cody Carpenter, a resonant synthesiser and piano piece that helps create the mood, mixed with some deliberately 1950s sci-fi sound effects during the birthing sequence. Overall the effects are notably gruesome with two exceptionally graphic headshots and the (mercifully) offscreen 'hoovering up' of Dr Kiefer's innards by an incensed Dwayne. Considering the incredibly tight two-week shooting schedules afforded to the Masters of Horror programmes there is quite a large amount of complicated prosthetic work on show.

Carpenter finally returned to feature filmmaking nearly ten years after *Ghosts of Mars* was released. He had taken his time to pick the right project.

> *'This was the first one that came along that had a small cast, a small budget and a reasonable shooting time in a simplified physical space. In other words, it all took place in one area [and] that was just right for me. That was what I was looking for.'*

> John Carpenter, *Empire online*, January 2011

The Ward (2010)

Directed by: John Carpenter
Produced by: Peter Block, Doug Mankoff, Mike Marcus, Andrew Spaulding
Written by: Michael & Shawn Rasmussen
Director of Photography: Yaron Orbach
Music: Mark Kilian
Starring: Amber Heard (Kristen), Lyndsy Fonseca (Iris), Mamie Gummer (Emily), Danielle Panabaker (Sarah), Jared Harris (Dr Stringer), Mika Boorem (Alice), Laura-Leigh (Zoey), Jillian Kramer (Monster Alice)
88 mins

> *'Something was in there. Something not right. Something not human...'*

Oregon, 1966. Kristen is picked up by the police after setting fire to a farmhouse. Although they feel that she should go to jail, Kristen is, in fact, packed off to the North Bend Psychiatric Hospital where the staff will ensure the right reception for their latest addition to the ward. Kristen is given her own room, that of previous inmate Tammy, and begins her timeless stay. She's determined to leave and even though the nurses, auxiliary staff and doctors seem professional they still treat her like the psychiatric patient they believe she is and that she is convinced she isn't. The other patients are also disturbed young women – friendly illustrator Iris, highly-strung Emily, vain Sarah and childlike, toy-rabbit-hugging Zoey. Dr Stringer is the psychiatrist whose job it is to treat these girls but Kristen is certain that she doesn't need help. Life in the institution is boring and monotonous until Kristen is attacked in the shower by a malevolent creature, a violent spirit that appears to haunt the ward. This has clearly happened before and the clues point perhaps to a reincarnation of the departed former patient Alice. There appears to be only one solution, a solution Iris has considered, as have the other patients – escape from the ward and the hospital, to get a glance once more at the real world – a world without demanding doctors, lecherous orderlies and varieties of pills, potions and random designs. But one by one the girls start to fall victim to the spirit, captured and killed in gruesome ways. Realising they could be next, Kristen and Emily make a move to escape, but they are prevented from doing so by the hideous creature. Can they ever get free or will the ward remain closed and the putrefied evil that has manifested in its sanctuary continue to apply its scurrilous necromantic designs on its victims?

The Ward is a well-defined horror film which, while it may not appear to be totally reminiscent of previous Carpenter outings, nevertheless explores similar styles to his earlier work. Modern audiences are now very used to seeing remakes of 1970s horror films and the 1966 setting of *The Ward* is contemporary in its design but is also a reference to the kind of films that many modern horror directors are using as an influence on current-day versions of classic horror flicks. In many respects this relationship to the new through references to the old is appropriate. It also means that Carpenter can use more traditional horror techniques without the film seeming outdated.

The Ward follows similar themes to those of *They Live* and *In the Mouth of Madness* in that the protagonists find themselves in a dangerous environment that is absolutely controlled by others and their only choices are to find a means of confronting it or escaping from it. *They Live* depicted a defined sci-fi context, *In the Mouth of Madness* was clearly horror/fantasy based, but *The Ward* keeps its cards much closer to its chest and evolves as a supernatural mystery. In a fully controlled environment the lead characters are initially sure of themselves and their actions but, as the film progresses, when they find they cannot convince others of their plight, they begin to have doubts about their sanity. Kristen is aware that her situation 'depends on whether you are ready to follow the rules' and it marks not only a sense of societal expectations within her community but also a confirmation of the dominance that those in charge have over her. Although the hospital and the ward are designed for mental treatment there is a noticeable concern amongst the group that 'you stay locked up long enough and you start to believe that you are nuts', and the new society that Kristen is part of has a clearly defined hierarchy. 'I'm not crazy,' she declares, only to be roundly informed that, 'We don't use that word here.' The society needs to conform to its own rules and language in order to function. It is only through the intervention of an outsider that the perceived normality can have any hope of changing.

The patients want one just thing – to depart the ward and go home. But their homes are not depicted to the viewer and neither are their relationships with anyone other than their fellow patients or the hospital staff. In the claustrophobic world of the ward it is their hobbies or perceptions that describe them, rather than their understanding of any possible environment that actually exists outside the hospital. But worse, even those who have left are not assumed to have departed for a better environment. The remaining girls discuss the circumstances of their former inmates' departures and pay attention to the details – 'If she went home why didn't she take her sketch pad?' is their response to Iris's demise. This in turn generates further concerns for themselves – 'If we don't get out of here we're next'.

The Ward's central character, Kristen, represents less the Carpenter Hawksian-style professional hero but rather an adept and confrontational protagonist who approaches her horrendous surroundings with skills seemingly learned from everyday life. Kristen has similar characteristics to those of *In the Mouth of Madness*'s John Trent with her curiosity (like Trent, she becomes a patient in a psychiatric institution) but she is perhaps more a modern version of *Halloween*'s Laurie Strode. Unlike Laurie, though, her past is not one that is creepily revealed as a plot device but rather one that is only partly and sporadically revealed to the viewer until the conclusion. Her background is not only not known to the audience but it also seems to be a confused record for her. Only Dr Stringer seems to know anything about her and although he's on hand to help with her treatment, he's not giving anything away. Laurie's connection to Michael in *Halloween* is but a small part of her story compared with Kristen's connection to herself, either in other people's perceptions, her own warped memory or the revelations of the increasingly twisted events that consume the ward and its inhabitants.

The question that most Carpenter fans are going to ask after such a long wait is: is it scary? Well, yes. Carpenter has returned to traditional techniques of eliciting scares from the viewer. He creates an environment that is utterly claustrophobic and then sets to work using this foetid atmosphere to generate the scenes of tension that pervade the movie, many of which are followed by sudden shocks. Although these don't match the masterful way in which they were employed on such classics as, say, *The Thing*, they are effective in creating the frights when they are needed. He offers a glimpse of modern horror trends, for example, showing us an array of surgical instruments that the spirit uses in order to dispatch another victim, which has the potential to head off into the realm of torture porn, but Carpenter wisely chooses not to pursue that particular strand of the genre, which focuses on excessive violence, pain and degradation. Yes, the scenes where the patients are dispatched are gruesome, but they are predominantly there for shock value, rather than dwelling on the suffering of the victims for any significant length of time. Additionally, the monster is revealed to the audience slowly – a technique that engages the viewer with tantalising glimpses but builds up the tension before it is depicted in its hideous gory glory. Hence we see an unknown attacker kill Tammy in the prologue, get a mere peek at the figure when Kristen is attacked in the shower, and so on, until Alice is eventually revealed to be a gruesome decomposing apparition. Carpenter doesn't fall into the trap of endlessly reviving the killer and instead opts for a denouement that provides an explanation derived from childhood trauma and fractured psychosis which is largely immaterial – *The Ward* is very much about the journey and not the destination.

The use of sound and music is notable for maintaining and advancing the action and, even though the score is not one of Carpenter's (he was involved and credited but most of the music was that of composer Mark Kilian), it is certainly one that enhances the atmosphere. At times it is mildly classical and ethereal but it also adds some rock and a hint of the sort of scores that graced early Dario Argento films. Sound is used to particularly good effect when creating additional stress and fear inside the ward and when horrific events either occur or threaten to. Kilian electronically manipulated ordinary everyday sounds but also used instruments like toy pianos as well as synthesisers to create a mood that augments the tension and emphasises the shocks.

The Ward is a good solid film, strong in its horror techniques and yet appropriate for a modern audience. And, importantly, it does deliver the scares.

OTHER PROJECTS

During the course of his career, Carpenter has been involved with a number of other projects, although not in the role of director. Many of the screenplays that he wrote early on in his career became feature films or TV movies. Later, once he had become established, he used his position to enable colleagues to get their own films off the ground, sometimes even appearing in these productions in cameo roles.

Eyes of Laura Mars (1978)

Directed by: Irvin Kershner
Produced by: Jon Peters
Written by: John Carpenter and David Goodman, from a story by John Carpenter
Cast: Faye Dunaway (Laura Mars), Tommy Lee Jones (John Neville), Brad Dourif (Tommy), Rene Auberjonois (Donald Phelps), Raul Julia (Michael)
104 mins

Our plucky heroine Laura has to beware the Eyes of Mars, not a thinly veiled reference to Julius Caesar but to her own unreleased book of photographs. Laura, you see, is an advertising photographer whose aggressive images appear on buses and in magazines all over the world. Deodorant has never looked so kinky. Her problem lies in the source of inspiration for her *chic sauvage* – occasional glimpses in dreams of real-life crimes whose post-mortem police photographs bear an uncanny resemblance to her own commercial offerings. This alone wouldn't be enough to provoke a police presence at her highly touted new exhibition, but the murder of Dora Spencer does. Still, the show must go on and Laura continues to shoot her 'violent and sexy photographs'. Meanwhile, her visions are becoming stronger as she sees through the eyes of the killer. Who could be responsible for these horrific acts?

Carpenter's script *Eyes* was optioned for big studio treatment while Carpenter himself was struggling up the ranks of low-budget film production. As is often the way with studio scripts, it was heavily doctored to fit a framework that suited them. Carpenter was apparently not impressed with the way that Columbia treated his work, claiming that it bore little resemblance to his original vision. But he has a co-screenwriting and story credit nevertheless. What remains is a cracking prime concept matched with a theme that revolves around voyeuristic obsession and its relationship with the camera. Ultimately this places *Eyes of Laura Mars* very much in the tradition of the Italian *giallo* films popular in the 1960s and 1970s – pulpy murder mysteries with convoluted, occasionally ludicrous solutions, bizarre situations, sex and violence, oodles of style and plenty of red herrings. Viewed in this context, and as a hybrid of Michael Powell's *Peeping Tom* (1960) and Michelangelo Antonioni's *Blow Up* (1966), *Eyes of Laura Mars* is perfectly satisfactory. Kershner's direction keeps things interesting, jumping from the glossy world of fashion to grimy, first-person, handheld work that characterises the killer's point of view. The photo shoots, in particular, as well as the photographs that they result in, stand out as gloriously tasteless kitsch, like a cross between JG Ballard and a Roxy Music album cover. In the final tally *Eyes of Laura Mars* is as shallow as the industry it reflects, but is watchable and enjoyable, remaining surprisingly unscathed in the years since its release, when many of its contemporaries look as dated as Tommy Lee Jones' hairstyle.

Halloween 2 (1981)

Directed by: Rick Rosenthal
Produced by: Debra Hill and John Carpenter
Written by: Debra Hill and John Carpenter
Director of Photography: Dean Cundey
Music: John Carpenter and Alan Howarth
Cast: Jamie Lee Curtis (Laurie), Donald Pleasence (Dr Loomis), Dick Warlock (The Shape), Charles Cyphers (Sheriff Bracket)
92 mins

'He's still on the loose.' About two heartbeats after the events in part one, pasty-faced nutter Michael Myers is back in action. Dr Loomis is, frankly, beginning to lose touch with reality – he even causes the death of an innocent bystander who looks vaguely like Myers. With all this mayhem going on it's hardly surprising that Haddonfield Hospital is doing heavy business, including its new patient, Laurie Strode, still feisty despite her horrendous experiences. But families like Laurie's keep close ties and, sure enough, her brother (shock revelation!) is keen to meet her again, even if it is outside of normal visiting hours. The stage is set for a long night of terror as a half-sedated Laurie must once again stand up to her estranged sibling who is carving out quite a name for himself in the Haddonfield Hospital of horror.

Slasher sequels, as *Scream 2* (1998) was so quick to point out many years later, have a simple rule: to feature more deaths than the original, and more elaborate ones at that. Using this criteria, *Halloween 2* fits the bill perfectly: the deaths are more frequent, more bloody and more convoluted. Sadly, the other rule about slasher sequels also applies: they are inevitably far less interesting than their forbears. Where *Halloween* played with the audience in terms of expectation and suspense,

Halloween 2 just drags after the opening murder until it reaches a tired selection of relatively tension-free but graphic slayings. In an attempt to bolster the concept that this is more scary (it isn't, it's just more violent) than its predecessor, the original score with its hypnotic rhythms has been remixed to become more 'rock 'n' roll' raucous, sounding more like Goblin's bombastic scores in Dario Argento's *Profondo Rosso* (1976) and *Suspiria* (1977). Unfortunately, Rosenthal is no Argento (indeed Carpenter, unhappy with the results, re-shot some scenes himself) and the images just can't compete with the soundtrack. There are some interesting touches in the script, notably the shock car-crash death, the decision to continue straight after the first film rather than 'a few years later...' and the riots outside the Myers' house that question mob mentality, but these are few and far between. Both Pleasence and Curtis look vaguely embarrassed by the proceedings; Curtis, in particular, had been typecast since her appearance in the original and was getting tired of these sorts of roles. As much as *Halloween 2* seeks to shock and entertain, it fails because it is limpid and bland. It was successful enough to demand another sequel, though.

Halloween III: The Season of the Witch (1982)

Directed by: Tommy Lee Wallace
Produced by: Debra Hill and John Carpenter
Written by: Tommy Lee Wallace
Music: John Carpenter and Alan Howarth
Cast: Tom Atkins (Daniel Challis), Stacey Nelkin (Ellie Grimbridge)
98 mins

Dr Daniel Challis is having a rough time. He has bought his kids some Halloween masks only to find that his ex-wife has already purchased some top-of-the-range latex ones from Silver Shamrock Novelties, whose irritating commercials lure children with the promise of a massive giveaway on Halloween night should they don their masks in front of the TV. To make matters worse, a toyshop owner called Harry Grimbridge is attacked in hospital and has his eyes squished out before the dispassionate murderer escapes only to flambé himself in his getaway car. There is some consolation, though; Challis teams up with Harry's hot daughter, Ellie, in an attempt to get to the bottom of the murder. Their destination is Santa Mira, an Irish town in California, the home of Silver Shamrock. But what has this to do with ancient pagan cults, the disappearance of part of Stonehenge and the fast approaching night of Halloween?

Carpenter and Hill made a conscious decision to move the *Halloween* franchise away from the endless stream of slasher rip-offs that followed in its wake. Writer/director Wallace had worked as editor and production designer on both the original *Halloween* and *The Fog* as well as being involved with art direction on *Assault on Precinct 13* so was part of the Carpenter circle. Story-wise, this is far from stalk 'n' slash territory and events unfold at a cracking pace – from the evocative, blue-lit opening where Harry ensures that a waxen-faced man who is attacking him is crushed between two cars to prevent him being strangled, right up to the shocking conclusion as our hero desperately tries to stop the slaughter. All of this is aided immeasurably by a superb Carpenter score that counterpoints the action and perfectly matches the computer-designed opening titles. This is a great little film which has sadly been brushed aside in favour of simpler, less challenging fare. Its horror, particularly in the scene where a family are killed in a controlled experiment, lies in the taboo realm of the film's potential victims – fifty million children. Sadly the film bombed at the box office and has been critically derided over the years.

The *Halloween* franchise, however, was not dead. Michael Myers was resurrected in increasingly tedious sequels featuring Donald Pleasence returning as Loomis in 1988, 1989 and 1995, the last of which – *The Curse of Michael Myers* – was one of

Pleasence's last performances. These three films had no further input from Carpenter or Hill other than a credit for creating the initial characters. The whole series was re-booted in *Halloween H20* (1998), which carried on the story 20 years after the original and saw Jamie Lee Curtis reprise her role (ignoring parts 4 to 6) in a fun, back-to-basics story from Steve Miner, a director who had made, ironically perhaps, two early episodes in the *Halloween* 'homage' series *Friday the Thirteenth*. Carpenter had been offered the opportunity to direct, but declined. Curtis, perhaps unwisely, returned in *Halloween Resurrection* (2002), directed by Rick Rosenthal, the director on the similarly unsatisfactory *Halloween 2*. This may have seemed like the end for the series but director Rob Zombie had other ideas, launching a 're-imagining' of the original film in 2007.

The Philadelphia Experiment (1984)

Directed by: Stewart Raffill
Produced by: Joel B Michales and Douglas Curtis
Executive Producer: John Carpenter
Story by: John Carpenter (uncredited in the film, credited on the trailer), Wallace Bennett and Don Jakoby
Written by: William Gray and Michael Janover
Cast: Michael Paré (David), Nancy Allen (Allison), Bobby DiCicco (Jimmy)
102 mins

'The Eldridge has vanished!'

Indeed it has. The SS *Eldridge* is part of a secret US Navy experiment – the Philadelphia Experiment – which cloaks water-bound vessels with an electromagnetic shield so that radar detection is rendered impossible. It's a vital tool in winning World War II. In 1943, sailors David and Jimmy are all set to mind the generators but something goes tragically wrong and a rift is created in space-time, linking to a similar experiment 40 years in the future. They find themselves wandering in a time they cannot comprehend, pursued by military personnel with equipment far superior to theirs. They kidnap the recently disenfranchised Allison at a grotty diner and soon Allison and David start to form a relationship. But Jimmy is not well, suffering strange electrical spasms. Before long he disappears, torn back in time, leaving Allison and David to piece the intervening years together and evade the military. With increased intensity of atmospheric disturbances and the breakdown of spatio-temporal verisimilitude in the vortoxial stream, both sides of the space-time continuum look pretty grim...

The Philadelphia Experiment is not so much *Back to the Future* (1985) as Forward to the Past – a jolly, Saturday-morning, sci-fi adventure film with all the trimmings of the genre. Carpenter originally planned this to be his next project after *Escape from New York*, but he felt that the story lost impetus after the time jump. However, the script was bought up and Carpenter given the role of executive producer on the shoot, where he approved the various script rewrites. In some ways his original concern with the film bears out in the final viewing. It starts wonderfully in 1943 and creates a real sense of intrigue when Dave and Jimmy find themselves in a hostile, helicopter-patrolled desert the other side of the vortex. Some aspects do seem very reminiscent of Carpenter projects: the kidnapped girl, the distrust of authority, Fortean phenomena, a possible apocalypse, man on the run, professionalism and the fragility of American cultural mores – they first suspect they have travelled forward in time and that America has lost the war when they find a discarded German beer bottle. Things fall apart in the middle third, which feels far too *Dukes of Hazzard* to gel properly. The romantic subplot doesn't really work, either, as David is basically a bullish, unsympathetic character. Another problem lies in the *Eldridge*'s return, with some of the crew still smouldering in man-machine fusion – it seems just a little grotesque for what is otherwise a gentle action-romance.

Ultimately, *The Philadelphia Experiment* is wholesome fun with a touch of romance, action, adventure, science fiction and nostalgia that holds the audience's attention for most of its running time.

Black Moon Rising (1985)

Directed by: Harley Cokliss
Executive Producer: John Carpenter
Written by: Desmond Nakano, William Gray and John Carpenter from a story by John Carpenter
Cast: Tommy Lee Jones (Quint), Linda Hamilton (Nina), Robert Vaughn (Ryland), Richard Jaeckel (Earl Wyndom)
100 mins

Black Moon – it ain't all black as there's that trendy red stripe, and it ain't the moon. Instead, it's a super-duper slick car and everyone wants it. Our hero? Quint. Wears black. Talks straight. He's got 72 hours to get the car and an important cassette he's hidden in it because he's working undercover for the government and you really don't want to mess with the government. You also don't mess with Nina, a tough cookie who specialises in pinching motors, and she wants Black Moon too. Quint messes with both, and ends up 'sleeping with the enemy'. This proves to be a good move, though, as Black Moon is changing owners at a frightening pace and sometimes teamwork is the best way to realise your goals...

Oh dear. *Black Moon Rising* is a classic example of how to take a solid thriller concept and turn it into mush. What sets most Carpenter films apart from their contemporaries is that they have aged very little. Sadly, this bears all the hallmarks of a mid-1980s action flick. Tommy Lee Jones looks ridiculous in his leather outfit and unfortunately the dialogue delivery – 'I'm getting too old for this' – lacks irony. When we first come across Quint he coolly prevents a convenience store robbery but, paradoxically, the next scene sees him stealing from a corporation – his efforts resulting in a bullet-riddled escape. This and much of the other action – fight scenes, car chases, etc – is filmed in such a lethargic manner you forget that there is anything going on at all. Couple this with a painfully bad sex scene (it's backlit and accompanied by a sax solo) and you are left wondering what on earth happened to create such a tedious mess. There are elements in the script that are Carpenter – the plot, some of the dialogue, mistrust of the authorities, double crossings and an increasingly beaten-up protagonist are reminiscent of his other work – but the bland, one-note direction and shocking levels of cheesy posturing render this a less of a car chase and more a car wreck of a movie. As a director, Carpenter can make periods of narrative inactivity captivating or insightful, but frankly this is as exciting as golf.

TV Movie Screenplays

Over the years, Carpenter has also found a number of his screenplays being optioned for TV movies of varying quality. Some of these were spec-scripts and others for projects he had intended for bigger things – to be shown on the big screen and directed by himself. Certainly, in the earlier scripts, there is a clear indication that Carpenter's initial ambitions as a director were not limited to the realms of the science-fiction, horror and action films he's most commonly associated with, but with a broader range of subjects.

Zuma Beach (Lee H Katzin [1978]) features Bonnie Katt (Suzanne Somers) as a rock singer in crisis. She decides to take a break from it all down on Zuma beach and ends up wowing the boys with her jiggly volleyball skills and inspirational sand-modelling techniques. Essentially a series of episodic encounters mixed with a nostalgic feel for Frankie Avalon beach movies of the 1960s (complete with retro soundtrack), this is diverting at best and features a very early screen role for Rosanna Arquette.

Better Late Than Never (Richard Crenna [1979]) concerns the occasionally comic activities that revolve around an old people's home and the arrival of a newcomer who is definitely not welcome. An escape bid is planned and the old folk end up stealing a train to get as far away as possible.

El Diablo (Peter Markle [1990]) was one of two westerns written in the 1970s. Co-written with long-time collaborator Tommy Lee Wallace (as well as Bill Philips), the plot concerns a school teacher out to rescue his kidnapped pupil from the devilish clutches of the notorious El Diablo. He can hardly shoot pool let alone a gun, so he hires a not-entirely-trustworthy crew of gunslingers. Mainly played for laughs, this won Carpenter a 1991 ACE Award for writing when it was finally produced.

Blood River (Mel Damski [1991]) was originally conceived in the mid-1970s as a western (presumably the title refers to Hawks's *Red River*) with two very specific stars in mind – John Wayne and gun-toting, TV-shooting, karate-kicking, wiggle-hipped Elvis Presley. Sadly, by the time the script was finally filmed both the Duke and the King had shuffled off this mortal coil. Jimmy Pearls (Rick Schroder) is on the run because he killed a bunch of people who murdered his parents for land. He befriends an old trapper (Wilford Brimley) who, unbeknownst to him, is hiding a dark secret. Of interest is former Mrs Carpenter Adrienne Barbeau starring as Georgina and Gary Kibbe's role as one of the cinematographers.

Silent Predators (Noel Nosseck [1999]) is a disposable and ludicrous horror. Twenty years ago a truck crash resulted in the release of the mightily deadly Eastern Diamondback snake into the wild and, wouldn't you know it, the blighter has been breeding in the intervening time. Now, thousands of wriggly death mongers are slithering their way to San Vicente for a quick bite in rather tedious, red blurry vision.

Computer Games

Sentinel Returns (1998)
Music: John Carpenter

Based upon Geoff Crammond's classic 8-bit computer game *The Sentinel*, this is strategy- based weirdness set across hundreds of 3-D checkerboard levels. The aim is to absorb the sentinel that stands vigilant watch over the land below by building boulders, creating robots and possessing them until sufficient height has been reached to stage a coup. To make matters more difficult, the sentinel is absorbing growths on the landscape, and that can include you! The game plays with an ominous, atmospheric John Carpenter soundtrack. Even if you are not a fan of computer games (*Sentinel Returns* is good) it is worth seeking this one out as it can be played as a standalone music CD (for the PC version) with six Carpenter tunes collectively entitled *Earth and Air* for you to enjoy, totalling about 23 minutes.

F.E.A.R 3 (2011)
Co-Story: John Carpenter

Annoyingly renamed *F3.A.R.* in an attempt, presumably, to give it an air of cool (it didn't work for Se7en and seems passé here), Carpenter was brought on board by comic artist Steve Niles to flesh out the game's dialogue. Carpenter, who enjoys video games, provided inspiration for the cinematics of the game. As gaming becomes increasingly aligned to high-end cinema, this form of approach to game development (which itself often has blockbuster $100-million budgets) will become increasingly common, and here the adoption of a named director seems prescient. F.E.A.R (First Encounter Assault Recon) offers the player a combination of first person shooter instant thrills with survival horror jumps and scares. The previous two incarnations of the game have offered tension and gore, a perfect combination that Carpenter, a master of tension, should be able to further improve upon.

THE MORE THINGS CHANGE,
THE MORE THEY STAY THE SAME:
THE LEGACY

MM: If you could pick which of your films was going to be remade, which one would you choose?
JC: The one where they pay me the most money.

John Carpenter's Business of Insanity
by Jason Matloff, 31 July 2007

The need for Hollywood to rely on branded or known products to sell its next 'big thing' is particularly rife in genre films, which are predominantly aimed at an audience who may only have heard of the original. In recent years, the interest in 1970s and 1980s genre films has led to a slew of remakes and Carpenter's output is ripe for plundering, along with contemporaries like George A Romero and Wes Craven. These new films – while acknowledging their forbears – are more about re-branding product to appeal to a contemporary aesthetic. This isn't just in the way the films deal with effects, pacing and soundtrack but also in the way that they approach story. Carpenter's strength as a writer lies in creating iconic, mythical stories that work in a plain, no-nonsense way. Modern scripting revels in providing (often unnecessary) subplot and backstory, informing the audience to the extent that they appear to be cleverer than they actually are. This is not necessarily a bad thing; it is a sign of the times and can add to the overall 'believability' of the plot. What it does mean is that the remakes of Carpenter's films tend to elaborate and expand on the originals, making for more complex stories but often at the expense of narrative simplicity and single-purpose drive.

The Fog (2005)

Directed by: Rupert Wainwright
Written by: Cooper Layne from a screenplay by John Carpenter and Debra Hill
Produced by: John Carpenter, David Foster and Debra Hill
Cast: Tom Welling (Nick), Maggie Grace (Elizabeth), Selma Blair (Stevie Wayne), DeRay Davis (Spooner)
100 mins

Antonio Island, home of happy, carefree townsfolk breaking out the bunting to celebrate the centenary of their community. Little do they know that their prosperity was built on betrayal and violence when the four men who founded the town sent William Blake's leper colony to their deaths on the waves, stealing their wealth and hushing up their terrible secret. The suppressed memories of that fateful day will come rolling in like the dense fog that is threatening to engulf Antonio Island, hiding in its bilious depths the ghosts of Blake and his people, eager to obtain vengeance from the descendents of those who betrayed them. One of those descendents is Nick Castle, whose girlfriend Elizabeth has recently returned to the island. All should be fine for the festivities but, as local commentator and lighthouse disc jockey Stevie warns, beware of the fog.

With Carpenter taking the producer's chair along with Debra Hill (who sadly passed away, aged 54, before the film was finished), the remake of *The Fog* sticks fairly close to its source script although writer Layne has embellished some of the flashbacks, removed the campfire bookending and introduced elements of additional research and escalation. The result is a far less economical film, one prone to exposition rather than atmosphere, but it does, for the most part, hold its own. In seeking a PG-13 rating in the US the film has plenty of nasty moments but is low on actual viscera – not necessarily a bad thing because, at heart, *The Fog* is a ghost story, a simple tale that doesn't need overt gore. It's been updated to include references to the Internet and other such modern trappings but effectively it could be set in an 'anywhen'. Director Wainwright reins in some of the excesses of his bombastic *Stigmata* (1999) and manages to elicit some eerie and striking moments; a dining table on the beach in the moonlight, a flaming man crashing through a room and, indeed, the ghost ship itself. Many of the underwater sequences are genuinely unnerving and otherworldly, especially impressive considering the film's relatively modest budget. Counteracting this, though, is a lack of tension, so memorable in the original and vital to maintaining the ghostly mood. Partly this is due to the needs of modern, fast-paced editing (contrast the lingering, tense shots of the original) and partly because the score interferes with the atmosphere of the film rather than complementing it. Another issue is that of the fog itself – it needs to be creepy and tactile but the excessive CGI fog feels more artificial and far less menacing. Still, *The Fog* is a passable entry in the horror genre with some effective scenes and impressive lighting.

Assault on Precinct 13 (2005)

Directed by: Jean-Francois Richet
Written by: James DeMonaco (based on the film by John Carpenter)
Cast: Ethan Hawke (Jake Roenick), Laurence Fishburne (Marion Bishop), John Leguizamo (Beck), Maria Bello (Alex Sabian), Gabriel Byrne (Marcus Duvall)

109 mins

Detroit, 31st January. Sgt Jake Roenick has been given the task of supervising the shutdown of Precinct 13. With harsh weather closing in, recently arrested arch crime boss Marion Bishop is unexpectedly diverted to Precinct 13 and must stay in the already full cells until he can be transferred out. However, Bishop has the low down on a number of dirty cops and could rat on them all in court. Corrupt police officer Duvall decides he must take action and holds Precinct 13 under siege – no one is to get out alive. The good cops inside the precinct must join forces with the criminals if they are to survive the night.

Eschewing Carpenter's minimalist plot, *Assault on Precinct 13*, like so many of its contemporaries, feels a need to embellish and explain. We are given a backstory for Jake – he survived a failed stakeout where two of his colleagues were killed – something he's reluctantly getting psychological support for. Surviving this siege will give him the motivation to 'get back on the horse' and continue his good work as a cop. The original film's premise involved a street gang taking a blood oath to avenge the death of their own, their shocking killing of a little girl providing the catalyst for the siege. Nothing so subversive here (you can't kill a kid in the noughties!) and so the plot has become more lucid and revolves around a corrupt officer ensuring – by any means necessary – that his various misdemeanours are not uncovered, resulting in a completely different story and moral stance. Of all the characters, Laurence Fishburne's Bishop (confusingly, Bishop was the cop in the original) bears the most similarities to his counterpart Napoleon Wilson. He is, of course, a criminal, but he keeps his head throughout the siege and maintains a sense of honour.

Assault on Precinct 13 works well as a standalone film and is probably the best of the Carpenter remakes. It's coherent, tense when it needs to be, and the performances are uniformly good but it's difficult to understand why they bothered to associate it with the original film.

Halloween (2007)

Directed by: Rob Zombie
Written by: Rob Zombie (based on the film by John Carpenter)
Cast: Malcolm McDowell (Sam Loomis), Sheri Moon Zombie (Deborah Myers), Tyler Mane (Michael Myers), Scout Taylor Compton (Laurie Strode)
109 mins

Haddonfield. Mask-obsessed Michael Myers' teacher notices that he has been occupying himself by killing animals and arranges for him to meet psychiatrist Sam Loomis. Michael is a disturbed lad who has had a deeply unhappy childhood so, come Halloween, he grabs a knife and goes about killing those who have upset him. His little sister survives. Years later, having spent most of his life in an institution, he has grown to enormous size and claims not to recall any of the events of his childhood. He is still, however, capable of murder – his victims include a nurse and even the friendly caretaker. When his mother kills herself, he escapes the institution and heads for Haddonfield, presumably, Loomis surmises, to find his sister, Laurie. Laurie has subsequently been adopted by the Strode family and intends to spend this Halloween babysitting…

Rob Zombie's 're-imagining' of *Halloween* feels obliged to explain the psychosis and backstory of its characters to such an extent it makes the re-make of *Assault on Precinct 13* feel decidedly lacklustre. We learn that Michael Myers' father was abusive, his mother a pole-dancer and that people treated him badly in a prologue that runs for over a third of the running time of the original film. Bizarrely, this extended backstory explains why he grows up to look like a pro-wrestler and goes round killing everyone. The point of Carpenter and Hill's Michael Myers was that he was creepy, enigmatic and almost supernatural. Zombie – almost apologetically – explains the reasons for his killing spree and, in doing so, completely demystifies the monster. Myers has ceased to be 'the Shape', a bogeyman upon which we can project our fears, and is instead turned into a clearly defined, thuggish serial killer. Rob Zombie's *Halloween* arrived in the wake of the 'painographic' (or 'gore-no') horror films of the noughties. Films such as *Hostel* and the *Saw* (2004 onwards) franchise took horror in a new direction, one that dwelled upon pain and suffering, a direction Zombie partly embraced but, through his love of classic 1970s horror, also rejected, preferring to maintain a grimier look to his work. Apparently he wanted to remake *Halloween* because it was a film that he genuinely loved. But what he fails to achieve is any degree of tension or even much shock value – both crucial elements in a horror film. Ultimately there is no empathy towards either Myers or his conveyor-belt victims – just suspense-free murders that are sadistic and prolonged but not imaginative, affecting or subversive. A film of sound intention that tries to reinvent the myth for a modern age while acknowledging its ancestry, it ends up as a flabby, scare-free chore.

Halloween 2 (2009)

Directed by: Rob Zombie
Written by: Rob Zombie
Cast: Malcolm McDowell (Sam Loomis), Sheri Moon Zombie (Deborah Myers), Tyler Mane (Michael Myers), Scout Taylor Compton (Laurie Strode)
105 mins

The commercial success of *Halloween* on the relatively modest investment meant a sequel was inevitable and, once again, Rob Zombie writes and directs. In a nod to the original *Halloween 2* the film opens directly after the events of the first film with a severely injured Laurie in Haddonfield hospital. Before long her brother is up to his old tricks again, butchering nurses, patients and security guards with wanton abandon as our plucky heroine painfully drags herself around the hospital and its grounds in an attempt to avoid a family reunion that would in all likelihood end in a bloody mess. This homage to the original *Halloween 2* works well as a short standalone piece (rather similar in tone to Carpenter's short *The Gas Station* in *Body Bags*) and contains enough killings, jumps and tension to maintain interest. However, this is but a prologue to the film, relayed as a dream/flashback from the psychologically scarred Laurie. It is now fast approaching the next Halloween and Laurie has an inkling that the butchery in Haddonfield is due to start again, especially considering Michael Myers' body was never found. Sure enough, as the big day approaches, so does Michael, slouching his way towards Haddonfield, dispatching all in his wake with ruthless, clinical efficiency and no trace of humanity in his cold eyes. Also in town is Dr Loomis, here not in the spirit of reconciliation but rather using the opportunity to cash in on the town's suffering by tastelessly plugging his book about Myers at the scene of some of the murders.

Loomis is definitely the character that has had the biggest overhaul here, in many ways more evil than Myers himself. Myers is psychotic whereas Loomis uses events in a cynical and calculated way to further his public persona and increase his book sales – he is totally unrepentant when he reveals details about Laurie's past in his book without having the decency to inform her first.

Once again Zombie uses a grainy, washed-out look to highlight the gritty seriousness of his film, and the violence is protracted and bloody (though a little less so second time around). The problem with the film is that – after the opening prologue – it all becomes rather monotonous, a matter Zombie tries to address by inserting dreamlike visions of Laurie's family, notably

Deborah Myers and a young Michael. These quickly descend into pretentious parody and seem to have been inspired by the TV series *Twin Peaks* and *Wild Palms*. *Halloween 2* did not replicate the box-office success of the first film although it did still turn a profit. A further sequel from the same stable seems unlikely but the popularity of the franchise means there's always a possibility of a further resurrection for the venerable series.

At the time of writing, plans for remakes or spin-offs of *Escape from New York*, *The Thing* and *They Live* are in the pipeline.

BIBLIOGRAPHY

Fischer, Dennis, *Science Fiction Film Directors*, McFarland & Company, North Carolina, 2000

Hardy, Phil (ed), *The Aurum Film Encyclopedia Horror*, Aurum Press, London, 1996

Muir, John Kenneth, *The Films of John Carpenter*, McFarland & Company, North Carolina, 2000

Newman, Kim (ed), *The BFI Companion to Horror*, Cassell/BFI, London, 1996

Sarris, Andrew, *Notes on the auteur theory in 1962* from *Film Theory and Criticism Introductory Readings*, Mast, Gerald and Cohen, Marshall, Oxford University Press, Oxford, 1985

Truffaut, François, *Hitchcock by Truffaut: The Definitive Study*, Paladin, London, 1984

Westfahl, Gary, *The Greenwood Encyclopedia of Science Fiction and Fantasy: Themes, Works and Wonders*, Greenwood Press, Westport, 2005

Wollen, Peter, *Signs and Meaning in the Cinema*, Indiana University Press in association with BFI Publishing, USA, 1972

INDEX

www.kamerabooks.com

→ **Accompanying DVD features 3 horror shorts**

→ **Looks at renowned directors, including Wes Craven, John Carpenter, David Cronenberg, Dario Argento, Sam Raimi and Hideo Nakata**

→ **For horror aficionados and media or film students**

Horror Films

Colin Odell & Michelle Le Blanc

The Kamera Book of *Horror Films* takes you on a journey into the realm of fear. From horror cinema's beginnings in the late nineteenth century to the latest splatter films, from the chills of the ghost film to the terror of the living dead, there's more than enough to keep you awake at night.

There's a whole world of terror to explore – Spanish werewolves, Chinese vampires, Italian zombies, demons in Britain, killers in America, evil spirits in Japan.

This book offers a guide to key films, directors and movements, including *Dracula, Frankenstein, Scream, Halloween, The Sixth Sense, Ringu* and *Evil Dead*, and the more unusual *The Living Dead Girl, Rouge, Les Yeux sans Visage, Nang Nak* and *Black Cat*.

978-1-84243-218-1   **£9.99**

www.kamerabooks.com

→ **Comprehensive and up to date look at cult director Dario Argento**

→ **Accessible introduction to a general readership of Argento's work – will also appeal to hardcore fan base**

Dario Argento
James Gracey

Hailed as one of horror cinema's most significant pioneers and the twentieth century's major masters of the macabre, Argento continues to create inimitable and feverishly violent films with a level of artistry rarely seen in the horror genre, influencing the likes of Quentin Tarantino, John Carpenter and Martin Scorsese. His high profile is confirmed with his role as producer on celebrated classics such as George A. Romero's *Dawn of the Dead* and Lamberto Bava's *Demons*. This Kamera Book examines his entire output, including his most recent film *Giallo*.

978-1-84243-318-8   £12.99

→ **Invaluable overview of the best Asian Horror titles currently available in the UK**

→ **Offers fascinating cultural background on the crucial role of the supernatural in Asian folklore, literature and theatre**

→ **Strong appeal to cult/horror fans and students of Asian cinema**

Asian Horror

Andy Richards

Since Japanese horror sensations *Ring* and *Audition* first terrified Western audiences at the turn of the millennium, there's been a growing appreciation of Asia as the hotbed of the world's most exciting horror movies. With scores of Asian horror titles now available to Western audiences, this Kamera Book helps the viewer navigate the eclectic mix of vengeful spooks, yakuza zombies, feuding warlocks and devilish dumplings on offer, discussing the grand themes of Asian horror cinema and the distinctive national histories that give the films their special resonance. Tracing the long and noble tradition of horror stories in eastern cultures, it also delves into some of the folk-tales that have influenced this latest wave of shockers, paying tribute to classic Asian ghost films throughout the ages.

978-1-84243-320-1   £12.99